North America

ATLANTIC OCEAN

M E X I C O

Gulf of Mexico

Hispaniola

Cuba

P A C I F I C   O C E A N

Gulf of Mexico

Guatemala

Honduras

Nicaragua

South America

Costa Rica

Panama

mpico

Gulf of Mexico

EL TAJÍN

DZIBILCHULTUN

Y U C A T Á N

CHICHÉN ITZÁ

MAYAPÁN

UXMAL

TULÚM

JAINA

REMOJADAS

TRES ZAPOTES

Comalcalco

LA VENTA

C A M P E C H E

M I X T E C A

V E R A C R U Z

Río Usumacinta

Río Grijalva

PALENQUE

PIEDRAS NEGRAS

UAXACTÚN

TIKAL

YAXCHILÁN

Lake Petén

P E T É N

MONTE ALBÁN

Oaxaca

MITLA

O A X A C A

BONAMPAK

C H I A P A S

S O C O N U S C O

G u a t e m a l a

QUIRIGUÁ

COPÁN

H o n d u r a s

KAMINALJUYÚ

El Salvador

ART

BY ANDRE EMMERICH

WITH PHOTOGRAPHS BY LEE BOLTIN

BEFORE COLUMBUS

The art of ancient Mexico—from the archaic villages of
the second millennium B.C. to the splendor of the Aztecs

Simon and Schuster/New York

ACKNOWLEDGMENTS

The author would like to acknowledge his debt of gratitude to all those whose help made this book possible. The many friends who freely shared their knowledge are too numerous to list, but thanks are herewith tendered to each. Particular mention is made of that generous friend and mentor, the late Miguel Covarrubias, for his early encouragement and his profound insights. Most especially, thanks are expressed to Dr. Gordon F. Ekholm of the American Museum of Natural History whose constant helpfulness and sage advice were invaluable. To the author's wife much is due for many important suggestions, thoughtful editing and unfailing support during the long months of the book's growth.

The success of Lee Boltin's photographic expedition to Mexico was made possible by the generous cooperation of the Instituto Nacional de Antropología e Historia in Mexico City. Thanks are expressed to the director, Dr. Eusebio Dávalos Hurtado, as well as to Señor Ikar Laurari for their extensive helpfulness. Many thanks are also due Dr. William R. Coe of the University of Pennsylvania Museum for making possible the visit to the University's Tikal Project in the Petén jungle of Guatemala. In addition the friendship and hospitality of Mr. and Mrs. Leon Davidoff contributed substantially to the happy results of this trip. Finally, grateful acknowledgment is made of the manifold courtesies extended by the Photographic Division of the American Museum of Natural History and its director, Mr. Robert Logan, and of the expert assistance of Mr. Alex Rota.

For ADAM, TOBY *and* NOAH EMMERICH
  and JULIA *and* BEN BOLTIN
in whose time
the answers to the remaining riddles
may be found

CONTENTS

INTRODUCTION

Pope Pius X once said that spiritually we are all Semites. It can be said with equal justice that aesthetically we are all Greeks, deriving our civilization's basic sense of beauty and perfection from ancient Greece by way of the Renaissance. From the Greeks too we learned the word "barbarian," which in its original meaning referred to all non-Greeks. The latter-day euphemism for barbarian is "primitive," a kinder but equally devastating condemnation. The term as it is commonly understood today is best illustrated by comparing it with baby talk—sweet, amusing, but only a crude attempt to speak the language of adults.

It was long felt that artists, to the degree that they differed from the Greek ideal of beauty and perfection, fell short of their goal and were "primitive." Because of this old attitude, the label "primitive art" continues to be attached to the art of the ancient cultures of the Americas. Although the discoveries and the impact of modern art have changed our view profoundly, it seems that the opprobrious term is not to be shaken off. Significantly, most of the museums in which great pre-Columbian collections are

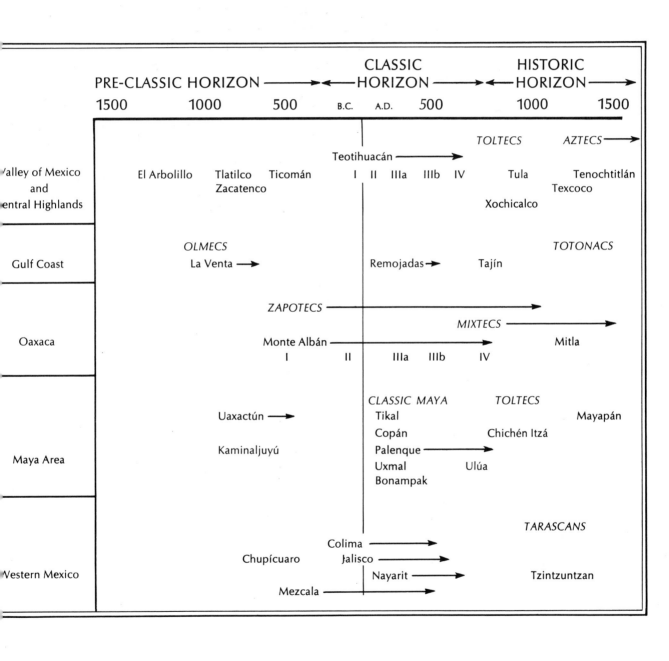

PRE-CLASSIC HORIZON ⟶ ⟵ CLASSIC HORIZON ⟶ ⟵ HISTORIC HORIZON ⟶

1500   1000   500   B.C.   A.D.   500   1000   1500

Valley of Mexico and Central Highlands

TOLTECS   AZTECS ⟶

Teotihuacán ⟶

El Arbolillo   Tlatilco   Ticomán   I   II   IIIa   IIIb   IV   Tula   Tenochtitlán
                 Zacatenco   Texcoco

                                                                                Xochicalco

Gulf Coast

OLMECS   TOTONACS
La Venta ⟶   Remojadas ⟶   Tajín

Oaxaca

ZAPOTECS ⟶

MIXTECS ⟶

Monte Albán ⟶   Mitla

I   II   IIIa   IIIb   IV

Maya Area

CLASSIC MAYA   TOLTECS

Uaxactún ⟶   Tikal   Mayapán

                              Copán   Chichén Itzá

Kaminaljuyú   Palenque ⟶

                              Uxmal   Ulúa
                              Bonampak

Western Mexico

TARASCANS

Colima ⟶

Chupícuaro   Jalisco ⟶

Nayarit ⟶   Tzintzuntzan

Mezcala ⟶

found, in this country and in Europe, are museums of natural history and ethnology rather than art museums. The Louvre boasts splendid Egyptian and Sumerian objects, but ancient American art is kept in the Musée de l'Homme. New York's Metropolitan Museum of Art conforms to the pattern and, until very recently, so did the other great American museums. The same is true of virtually all the museums of Germany, Italy, the Netherlands, Belgium, Austria and Switzerland. The most splendid achievements of pre-Columbian art are all too often stacked in crowded cases next to such workaday finds as spearheads, tools and potsherds, all lumped together in ethnographic exhibits.

Pre-Columbian finds do include some exceptionally early objects which could be called "primitive" if the word is taken in the sense of archetype or early prototype, although the term "archaic" is preferable and more accurate. But the fine pre-Columbian art works that we are acquainted with were made by extremely sophisticated artists. They embody all the subtleties and refinements of countless generations of artisans. They are the proud expression of one of the world's great ancient civilizations. The splendor of this art was recognized by Albrecht Dürer in the sixteenth century, but this did not save the gold and silver objects he so admired from the melting pot. Glorious turquoise mosaics were broken up as *"ornamenti dei barbari"* so that their stones could be reset in the Florentine workshops of the Medici, who had received them as gifts from the Spanish court. Only in our own time has pre-Columbian art begun to be understood once again.

That an approach to art and beauty other than the one inspired by the Greek ideal is possible was first realized by pioneering modern artists at the turn of this century. Painters like Picasso, sculptors like Lipchitz and Brancusi, found that the extraordinary objects from faraway places exhibited in the ethnographic museums or sold in curio shops were works by artists who were concerned with the same aesthetic problems as those with which they themselves were concerned. They began to collect the pieces they admired; the objects still cost very little, since so few collectors were interested in them. Then, slowly, as the vision of these pioneers filtered down the pyramid of taste, more and more people began to share their enthusiasm. But this art still is called "primitive," with insistent implication that it is necessarily inferior to the art that conforms to European traditions.

In Mexico, among the first to rediscover pre-Columbian objects as works of art were the famous Mexican painter Diego Rivera, the Frenchman Jean Charlot, the Austrian Wolfgang Paalen, and the late artist-archaeologist Miguel Covarrubias. André Breton in France and Henry Moore in England, among others, felt its compelling force, and the grand exhibition of pre-Columbian art which the Mexican government sent on a European tour in 1952 spread this enthusiasm throughout the Continent. In this country, the growing collections of pre-Columbian art in such museums as the Cleveland Museum, the Chicago Art Institute, the Worcester Museum, and the Virginia Museum of Fine Arts, the Bliss collection in the National Gallery of Art, the many special exhibitions of pre-Columbian art and the ever-increasing number of collectors, all have demonstrated our generation's response to the art of the great ancient cultures of America.

The history of pre-Columbian archaeology is almost as short as that of the appreciation of pre-Columbian art. The splendid ruins of Maya cities were sketched, photographed, and even copied with plaster casts, during the second half of the nineteenth century. But it was not until 1902 that Zelia Nuttall noticed the difference between Aztec remains and the objects found underneath the ancient lava bed on the outskirts of Mexico City. The first systematic explorations followed in 1909, when Manuel Gamio, who has been called the "father of Mexican archaeology," began to make scientific excavations in the Valley of Mexico. Among the important explorers who followed him were Mexicans, like Alfonso Caso, Frenchmen, Swedes, Germans and Americans, including George C. Vaillant, who did so much to uncover and classify the earliest known cultures of Mexico.

How recent much of our knowledge is in this field is demonstrated by the story of the search for the remains of the Olmec culture, now recognized as the great mother culture of Middle America. The first surface exploration of the lower Gulf Coast region, where many of their great temple-city ruins have been excavated, was made in 1925 by Frans Blom and Oliver La Farge. Large-scale excavations did not begin until 1938. The famous jade cache at Cerro de las Mesas was found in 1940. Not until 1955 did Philip Drucker excavate the group of jade figurines at La Venta and, still later, the mosaic floors and other material, which have been dated, by radioactive measurements, at about 800 B.C. Until that time the culture had been dated a full thousand years later, and its importance had been suggested only by the unsubstantiated and often criticized theory of Miguel Covarrubias. Still more recently, there has been discovered a remarkable, highly developed sculptural style which flourished in the Guatemala highlands as early as 500 B.C. and whose significance in relation to our picture of early cultural development has not yet been fully evaluated.

The constant possibility that new finds will open up vast new areas of knowledge is one of the things which lend so much drama and excitement to the unfolding story of American archaeology. Many pieces of the puzzle are still missing, but almost every year some are found. Few great archaeological surprises are likely to be found in Egypt and Greece, but in Middle America we stand on the threshold of some of the greatest discoveries. Bit by bit the picture becomes more nearly complete as great art treasures continue to be found. The murals of Bonampak discovered in 1947 and the fabulous clay sculpture which began to come out of Veracruz some four or five years ago are among the many recent examples.

In looking at pre-Columbian art, especially in some of the more old-fashioned and under-financed ethnographic and natural history museums, it is important to remember that they were all created in tropical latitudes where the sun stands high in the sky all year and sends down its dazzling light at an acute angle to walls and statues. This makes even very shallow bas-relief stand out with brilliant clarity. In the diffuse northern light, and especially in poorly illuminated museum cases, such vital details are sometimes barely visible. Fortunately, the bright high sun of Mexico can be replaced with a strong floodlight, and the ancient sculpture can once again come to life with undiminished force.

To understand and appreciate the art of the ancient Indian cultures it is important also to know the story of how they began, came to flourish and eventually declined. This book traces the history of the many peoples who lived in Middle America and contributed to its civilization, and whose presence in history is so splendidly mirrored in the art they left behind.

Two great focal centers of high civilization developed in the Americas. One was in Middle America, in the highlands of Mexico and Guatemala and in the lowlands surrounding them; the other was in South America, in the central Andes and in the coastal stretches of Peru. From both centers, satellite cultures spread to other places, including the southern part of Central America, where influences from Mexico and Peru met. Along the periphery of the great centers were other population groups, which remained fossilized in various earlier stages of development. These barbaric peoples exerted constant pressure on the great culture centers. Some of the more primitive groups learned enough from their more advanced neighbors and became strong enough to invade the centers of civilization. This resulted in repeated periods of darkness followed by the rise of new cultures.

In Middle America, Indian civilization reached its very highest development and had its proudest achievements in astronomy, mathematics, calendar notation, hieroglyphic and rebus writing, as well as the major arts of architecture, sculpture and mural painting. Here too, individual artists often transcended the limitations of their time and traditions to create works of art that bear the mark of genius. In contrast, as Miguel Covarrubias has pointed out, the artists of the Peruvian cultures relied far more on technique and craftsmanship alone and remained always within the limits of traditional routine, aiming for the production of luxury objects of the highest workmanship but rarely creating a unique, individual work of art. The achievements of ancient Peruvian artists were often extraordinarily fine, but those of the artists of the Middle American cultures have an unequaled scope and a universal human impact. Artistic and, particularly, sculptural talent was abundant here as it has been in few other parts of the world. What is more, it was given especially wide and often free reign. Thus, for the three thousand years of its pre-Hispanic history Middle America in its world fulfilled a role comparable to that of the Nile, that of the Euphrates valley, or that of Greece, in the ancient Mediterranean world.

The history of Middle America has been divided into three basic periods. The first is the Preclassic Period, often also called "archaic," which encompasses the early village cultures as well as the incipient stages of the theocratic city-states which achieved their full development during the next period. The culture of the Preclassic Period flowered earlier in some places than in others and it continued to flourish in enclaves, as in western Mexico, long after it had disappeared elsewhere. Generally, however, the time span assigned to this horizon stretches from about 2000 B.C. to 200 B.C.

The great Classic Period, which follows next, was the age of priests. Its achievements include the temple-cities of the Maya, as well as Teotihuacán, Monte Albán and many other sites famous for their grandiose architecture and the splendid work of their sculptors, painters and astronomers. This period began about 200 B.C. and continued until one after another of the Classic cities was abandoned or destroyed between A.D. 650 and A.D. 900.

The last of the three basic horizons is properly called the Historic Period, because events which occurred during this time are recorded in written Indian history. The period begins with the collapse of the theocratic world of the Classic Period and introduces a new age of warriors and military empires. It is generally dated from the great invasion of the Valley of Mexico by the Toltecs in the early years of the tenth century and the cessation of the use of the complex "Initial Series" calendric notations in the Maya area. The period continues up to 1521, when Cortes and his followers destroyed the Aztec capital of Tenochtitlán, on whose site Mexico City now stands. The conquest of the rest of Mexico and Central America followed soon after.

NOTE
In the spelling of the names of Indian sites it should be remembered that, while all names are to be pronounced exactly as they are spelled, the Spanish x used in so many Indian names is pronounced as *sh*. For example, "Xólotl" is pronounced *sho'lotl*, "Xipe" is *she'pay*, "Uxmal" as *oosh-mahl'*. The only important exception is "Oaxaca," which is pronounced *wah-hah'kah*.

THE FIRST INHABITANTS

AT FIRST THERE WAS THE LAND, uninhabited by man. Its wide and endless reaches and the promise of its untapped plenty beckoned as invitingly to the paleolithic Siberian hunters as they would, some twenty-five thousand years later, to the Pilgrim Fathers. The prehistoric immigrants came to America across the land bridge which then connected Siberia and Alaska, perhaps some twenty-five thousand years ago. These first Americans still lived on an early Stone Age level. They slept in caves or in shelters of the most primitive kind, and they hunted wild animals with the help of dogs, their only domesticated animals. Their weapons were darts tipped with splinters of bone and stone. Moving from hunting ground to hunting ground, they penetrated as far as the southernmost tip of South America.

Very early traces of man have been found by archaeologists in many parts of the United States, in Alaska and in South America. The names of the sites where important finds have been located and explored have been given to the various types of hunting and plant-gathering cultures which have been defined; Folsom, Sandia,

Clovis and Cochise are among the best-known. Another important find was made in 1947 by the anthropologist Helmut de Terra at Tepexpán near Mexico City. Here were found the remains of an imperial mammoth killed with flint-tipped weapons and, nearby, the bones of the "Tepexpán man," who has been dated about 9000 B.C. Other groups of men lived on the shores of the sea, fishing and collecting mollusks. Huge shell middens that have been found at Cerro Mongote in Panama, on the coast of Chile, and as far south as the caves of Palli Aike near the Strait of Magellan, have been dated by the American explorer and archaeologist Junius Bird back to 7000 B.C. An elementary level of human existence, which did not even boast the invention of pottery, continued for thousands of years at the outer edges of the great Indian civilizations—as, for example, the Athapascans of the Yukon, the Tehuelches of Patagonia and the peoples of the Tierra del Fuego.

These early hunters and gatherers must have led a very hard, uncertain and dangerous life. Since they were constantly moving from hunting ground to hunting ground, the tribespeople could accumulate only such property as could be carried on their backs, and their society was limited to their own small clan. All others were enemies and bitter competitors for game and good territory. The plant-gathering tribes could hardly have been much better off. Their scanty food supply and the tremendous effort needed to gather an adequate daily ration did not leave them the energy to develop beyond the most elementary stages.

Then somehow, somewhere, a revolutionary discovery was made: the seeds of plants could be saved and later sown, to reproduce each its own kind. Thus, instead of having to depend on the chance finding of edible plants after laborious searching, these first farmers now could themselves determine where their food was to grow; and so they could plan their lives, as they did their food supply, months ahead. The most important plant cultivated was maize, Indian corn; it is still a mystery how this plant was developed from the wild grasses from which it is derived. By 2000 B.C., however, it was being widely planted all over Middle America. Some time later it was followed by the other important food plant, beans. These provided rich proteins to complement the starchy corn diet, and together the two commodities provided the physical basis for the great impetus of surplus energy which produced an extraordinary cultural development.

One of the tantalizing gaps in our knowledge is how and where the nomadic hunters and gatherers became the settled people who, with their excellent pottery and highly developed arts, are the earliest civilized people known to have inhabited Middle America. Few remains have been found of truly archaic cultures; the earliest known sites in this region are all too highly developed to represent the fascinating first steps of a new-born civilization. Middle America possesses no such relics as have been preserved, for example, in the bone-dry desert valleys at Huaca Prieta, in Peru, where remains have been found of a coastal people who date back as far as 3000 B.C. Of those early settlers we know that they depended mainly on shellfish and seafood supplemented at first by gathered and later by planted vegetables such as squash, gourds, chillies and beans; and that they had flaked-stone scrapers and knives and wove simple cloth. But they did not make pottery. One of the most fascinating discoveries made at Huaca Prieta, at another of Junius Bird's excavations, was that of two little gourds decorated with highly stylized human masks. These have been dated as of before 2000 B.C. and are the earliest known works of art in America.

The absence of comparable early remains in the valleys of Mexico has been attributed by Professor Paul B. Sears, of Yale, to the fact that during this period the high plateau of Mexico was studded with large, deep lakes. The earliest farmers lived around these lakes, which have left many ancient pebble beaches high up on the mountainsides of the valleys. The human remains, however, the artifacts, burials and refuse heaps, have long since been washed down into the valley basins and have been covered by many deep layers of silt. It is, of course, possible that careful future explorations of these ancient beaches will produce some valuable evidence relating to the life of the first permanent settlers.

The single most valuable tool in dating accurately the first evidence of man in America, as well as the later achievements of the great Indian cultures, has been a by-product of the discovery of atomic fission; it is called Carbon-14 dating. This was developed in 1950 by the atomic physicist Dr. Willard F. Libby, who used the principle that all living matter contains nitrogen atoms which are transformed by cosmic radiation into an unstable radioactive isotope called Carbon 14. This process comes to a stop with death, and thereafter the remaining radioactivity of the isotopes contained in organic matter is lost at a constant, regular rate which can be measured in a laboratory. Thus the age of such archaeological finds as charcoal, wood, textiles, teeth, bones, ivory, shells and food remnants can now be measured. At first, Carbon-14 dating entailed a margin of error of some 250 years either way, but now this margin has been reduced to only sixty years.

Carbon-14 dating opened extraordinary new perspectives to American archaeologists. Until the development of this method, for example, the whole development of the Middle American cultures was thought to have taken place during the short time span of fifteen hundred years between the birth of Christ and the Spanish Conquest in 1521. Today we know that the early ceramic cultures go back to 2000 B.C. and before. This has expanded the archaeological horizon to encompass a period of more than 3,500 years.

THE VILLAGE ARTISTS

Notes on all the photographs begin on page 238

THE EARLIEST KNOWN VILLAGE settlements have been found in the highlands near Guatemala City at a place called Las Charcas, and in the Valley of Mexico close to the modern villages of El Arbolillo and Zacatenco, just outside Mexico City. Around 2000 B.C. these villages of perhaps some two hundred people each were nestled along the shore of the great lakes which filled the center of the highland valleys. Their inhabitants lived a simple peasant life in an idyllic setting. The lakes provided splendid fishing, and the surrounding forest yielded plenty of game—deer, rabbits, wild fowl and other animals—which they hunted with small javelins of a type known as *atlatl*, still in use in Aztec times. Possibly they also raised and fattened dogs, which were an important source of meat to them in a world without cattle, sheep, pigs, goats or horses.

It is probable that the making of pottery was the province of women in these early times. Without a potter's wheel (which none of the pre-Columbian cultures had), they modeled bowls and characteristic long-necked jars of perfect roundness and simple, elegant forms. These are generally of only one color, ranging from black to coffee color, sometimes decorated with incised geometric designs and then patiently burnished with a piece of bone or agate to give the surface a deep, richly glowing luster. Many beautiful examples have survived, thanks to the custom of burying the dead with large quantities of objects, some merely symbolic and others intended for use in the next life.

Their most important, and by far most interesting, gifts to their dead consisted of large groups of small clay figurines. Delicately and expressively made, they generally represent young women, but later ones include a large variety of subjects, such as mothers with babies, girls holding puppies, warriors, ballplayers, acrobats, magician-priests, and even one touching portrayal of a man and woman embracing on a bench.

There has been considerable speculation as to the significance of the figurines. The best answer so far seems to be that they were ritual objects of an agricultural fertility cult, the earliest manifestation of religion as well as of art. Variations of these small, solid votive female figurines have been found at the earliest levels all over Middle America, from Honduras in the south to Chupícuaro in western Mexico, indicating a very wide diffusion of this early village culture.

The pioneer American archaeologist George C. Vaillant was the first to study these early cultures, and to classify the different varieties of votive figurines. To label them he used the letters of the alphabet from *A* to *K̇*, then further subdivided some groups, using numbers, as "C-9," "D-3," "H-4." Later, Miguel Covarrubias charted the development of these figurines, showing clearly how during the fifteen centuries from about 2000 B.C. to 500 B.C. one type evolved out of another, and different styles crossbred to produce still others.

The practical—if not very poetic—letter-and-number labels continue to prove their usefulness in scientific studies. Collectors generally use the more expressive single term "archaic," when referring to the art of the Preclassic Period; but archaeologists frown upon it, for the good reason that these sophisticated village cultures

are not truly archaic, and they insist that the term should be reserved for the developmental stage between the early hunters and gatherers and these relatively late, fully developed village cultures. But, since so few traces of this truly archaic period have been found, "archaic" continues to be widely used despite the scientific disapproval.

The early village culture spread over an enormous area, encompassing most of Mexico and Guatemala. Not unnaturally the level of its attainments was far from being uniform. Certain sites produced only a few figurines of a fairly crude sort, while others developed styles of extraordinary refinement and beauty. The highest level of all was reached by a large village at the site of a modern brickyard on the outskirts of Mexico City bearing the surprisingly appropriate name of Tlatilco ("where things are hidden"). The most beautiful figurines and pottery from this period have been found here, and for years this brickyard was the great hunting ground for Mexican collectors.

It was the late 1940s that workers in the brickyard began to find the strange objects in the clay they used in making bricks. Perceptive collectors and scholars soon took to visiting these brickyards every Sunday to buy the week's finds from the local workmen. At that time, one could get, for ten to fifty cents, the most splendid objects that today fetch hundreds of dollars on the international market. Finally, a full-fledged scientific excavation was carried out under the direction of Miguel Covarrubias, and some two hundred burials were unearthed with all their elaborate offerings, all of which were carefully studied and analyzed. It is from them that we derive our detailed knowledge of the happy life led here during the apogee of the village cultures.

The figurines of Tlatilco represent chiefly young girls with slim waists, small breasts and large, sometimes almost bulbous thighs. They seem to be the same physiological type of woman that appealed to early man in all parts of the world. The same form appears in the cave paintings of North Africa and Europe, and in such famous figurines, dating from the dawn of history, as the Venus

of Willendorf found some years ago in Austria. The arms and feet of Tlatilco figurines are generally stylized and abbreviated into an elegantly simplified abstraction which is a characteristic convention shared by many of the Preclassic cultures. The face, on the other hand, is always exquisitely modeled with a refinement and sensitivity amazing in such small figurines, which are rarely more than four or five inches tall. It is with justice that the D-1 type of figurine typical of Tlatilco was called the "Pretty Lady" type by the early collectors.

The women of Tlatilco are often shown nude, but as is usual in most Middle American cultures, without indication of genitals. Some figurines are represented with short skirts, some of which were made of woven textiles, others of grass fibers, while still others wear elaborate leggings made up of rattles of a type still worn by Indian dancers in remote parts of Mexico. Dressed or nude, all of the women of Tlatilco are shown with elaborate hairdresses. They wore their hair in long tails falling over the bosom, or running down the back, or wound around the head with beads and decorations, often topped by a turban or a small sombrero. They also wore elaborate collars, necklaces and earrings. Many figurines still preserve traces of red and yellow paint which clearly indicate the elaborate body painting practiced by the people of Tlatilco. There is additional evidence of this in the finely carved clay stamps found here, both of the flat and the round roller type. These seals were used to decorate textiles as well as body surfaces, probably with a dye made from the dried bodies of the cochineal insect.

An important symbolic expression is found in some of the figurines and also in occasional clay masks: the double-headed or double-faced personification of duality. There are little two-headed figurines that look like Siamese twins, while others, reminiscent of Picasso, have one head with three eyes, two noses and two mouths so that they can be seen simultaneously in profile and full face. Another manifestation of the same idea is a mask whose left side shows a live face and whose right side shows a skull.

This basic concept of duality persists through all of the later cultures and is of fundamental importance to the Indian view of the condition of men and gods. It continues to be expressed in the many double figures found in the art of the Classic and Historic Periods, in the worship of the planet Venus, which in its cycles is both morning star and evening star, and in the dual nature of the gods in the elaborate pantheon of Maya and Aztec times, where each divinity is possessed of both good and evil aspects.

Except for the occasional figures of shamans, no manifestations of ceremony are known at Tlatilco, although there is some evidence of human sacrifice in certain burials. It is also thought that the offerings of clay figurines to the dead (as many as one hundred have been found in a single grave) are a symbolic substitute for human sacrifice, replacing the servants and women who at other times were killed to accompany dead notables on their journey to the afterlife.

The aesthetic excellence of Tlatilco is reflected also in the quality of its superb ceramics. Innumerable beautifully made bowls have been found, as well as tall vases with elongated necks, stirrup-spout vessels of the type common in Peru, and sculptured effigy bowls representing fishes, ducks, monkeys, rabbits, and even men. Their human and animal forms were adapted to the utilitarian function of the vessels with great technical skill and sculptural imagination. They are typified by particularly sure, flowing forms heightened by firm, incised lines. Some of the most beautiful of the Tlatilco vessels, elegant eggshell-white bowls, were made of fine kaolin, from which porcelain is now produced.

Slowly, over the centuries, the population increased in the Valley of Mexico, and communities like Tlatilco along the shore of the great lake which filled the center of the valley grew and multiplied. Their agriculture developed, and so did the domestic arts. They succeeded in domesticating all of the important plants which formed the basis of Indian life through the centuries, many of which were unknown in Europe and whose introduction into the life of our own ancestors proved to be a great boon: maize and

chili, cotton, tobacco, tomatoes, cocoa. They also cultivated beans and squashes; and from the great maguey cactus they tapped the sweet syrup which ferments and become a fairly strong alcoholic drink called *pulque*. Still drunk widely in Mexico, this beverage looks like milk and has a slightly sour, refreshing taste.

Their agricultural technique, which unfortunately still persists in many parts of Latin America, was the so-called slash-and-burn system, whereby a patch of land is cleared, seeded, and harvested for a couple of seasons, and then, when the never-fertilized soil is exhausted, is abandoned to nature, while men go on to the next patch of land. Along with this, the early villagers developed a brilliant agricultural system which still survives in the "floating gardens" (*chinampas*) of Xochimilco near Mexico City. This system calls for the construction of large rectangular floats of interwoven reeds and branches, which are heaped with mud from a shallow lake bottom. This is then planted with rapidly growing, long-rooted plants, which quickly anchor the float. The resulting garden is automatically irrigated by the lake below and there is never a need to water it. To maintain the fertility of these amazingly productive gardens all that is necessary is to drag up some fresh rich mud from the lake bottom and spread it over the old soil. In this way, entire shallow lakes were covered with floating islets, with narrow canals in between, to serve as convenient roadways for the canoes that carried the farmers and their produce.

As their level of existence and comfort improved, so did the quality of their pottery and figurines. Specialization had become possible, and the most talented of the villagers were now able to devote all of their time to the making of fine pottery and votive figurines, with brilliant results. Between about 1000 B.C. and 500 B.C., the artists of Tlatilco and of a few other sites—such as Santa Cruz on the Rio Cuautla, near Cuernavaca, in the lush valley of Morelos—reached a level of technical accomplishment and aesthetic sophistication that was hardly ever equaled again by any of the great later cultures. One reason may have been that never again were artists permitted to follow their own inventiveness and record their direct impressions without having to submit to outside interference. During later centuries an increasingly rigid religious symbolism developed, and the arts were forced to follow increasingly rigid canons of ritual forms, to portray with always stiffer symbolism the elaborate pantheon of gods imagined by the hierarchy of priests who came to power during the next age. Only in the remote regions of western Mexico—in Jalisco, Colima and Nayarit, on the Pacific Coast, where village cultures persisted for a thousand years after they disappeared elsewhere in Middle America—were artists able to continue in their craft without the interference of priestly dictates. In this isolated area the old tradition was maintained and elaborated, and artists continued to produce direct, personal images of life as they experienced it.

THE ENDURING VILLAGES

THE FIRST OF THE WESTERN VILLAGE cultures and the farthest outpost of Preclassic civilization has been found at Chupícuaro, in the state of Guanajuato, northwest of the Valley of Mexico. It was a highly accomplished local culture, with strong affinities with the cultures of the central highlands, and it is dated at about 500 B.C. Since 1948 the site has been covered by a lake created as part of a flood-control project; but, before the inundation, some four hundred burials were excavated and studied.

The most characteristic aspect of Chupícuaro is the sympathetic style of its votive figurines. Unlike those of Tlatilco and the other centers to the south, the small Chupícuaro figurines are not modeled in the round but fall into the category of "gingerbread figurines." They look as if they had been cut out of a flat sheet of clay on which facial features, headdresses, necklaces, bracelets, and so forth, were then added in the form of little clay pellets, which were further refined with a small wooden modeling stick. Mexican archaeologists have given this technique the descriptive name *pastillaje*—that is, "pilling."

Chupícuaro figurines have been classified as the H-4 type in the Vaillant system and are easily distinguishable by their unique and expressive characteristics: long, heavily slanted eyes and a pronounced aquiline nose. Equally typical are the elaborate, finely detailed headdresses, necklaces, bracelets and what appear to be rosettes worn on sandals or tied to the ankle, and which are peculiar to the figurines of Chupícuaro. They are made of a buff-colored clay, which was colored, after firing, with red and white paint, of which unfortunately only a few traces generally remain. The people of Chupícuaro made both smaller and larger figurines than those found at other sites; there are exquisitely modeled figures as small as an inch high, while a few reached what for solid clay figures is the extraordinary height of twelve inches.

Along with the representation of young girls—here as elsewhere the dominant theme of the early votive clay figurines—other subjects were found, including boys, men, children with animals, and mature, very full-bosomed women, shown either standing or seated in a cross-legged position. They are unique in Preclassic art and seem to represent nursing mothers as personifications of abundance and fertility. The fascination with the full bosom also extended

into pottery; in one extraordinary variety of the typical Preclassic tripod bowl made here, each of the three supports realistically reproduced the form of a full breast. This brings to mind the Greek legend which relates how the first bowl was made from a mold of the bosom of Venus.

The pottery of Chupícuaro generally stands out because of its ample, luscious shapes and the technical excellence of its richly burnished surfaces, which range from light brown to near black. At a slightly later stage Chupícuaro also produced some of the earliest polychrome pottery known in Middle America, with geometric and basket-weave designs shown in black and white against a red background. Typical designs also include chevrons, crosses, diamonds, zigzags and stepped lines. On some bowls they are combined with subtly raised representations of a human face.

Close to this polychrome pottery in technique and spirit are the relatively rare hollow human figurines also found at Chupícuaro, standing some nine to twelve inches in height. Their stylized representations of men and women are heavily decorated with elaborate black-and-white geometric designs on a red background and, like the pottery bowls, they were burnished to a rich glow before firing.

The culture of Chupícuaro appears to have been a direct ancestor of the farther western village cultures, which have become famous for their extraordinarily large and aesthetically exciting production of clay sculpture. These belong to the Preclassic horizon in spirit and style, and they seem to have continued their archaic traditions as a cultural enclave for centuries after they were abandoned elsewhere. The whole complex of social and religious ideas which went into the formation of the theocratic Classic Period appears to have bypassed them. Highland influences do not seem to have penetrated until well into the tenth century, when Toltec and Mixtec styles began to replace the traditions of the village artists. For twelve or fifteen hundred years these cultures maintained their independence and continued to evolve the lively, imaginative forms with which their artists so sensitively expressed every aspect of their village life.

Strangely enough, notwithstanding their fabulous richness in archaeological material, these cultures have never been thoroughly studied. Little is known of their chronological associations or their social and religious pattern outside of what can be inferred from the innumerable examples of their pottery and figurines. They left behind no hieroglyphic writing, no recorded dates, no monumental architecture of dressed and carved stone. But in their marvelously realistic "genre art" which was buried in abundance in the finely built, deep-chambered tombs of their notables they have left behind a richly detailed, anecdotal record of the simple, settled life of their villages.

These cultures are generally divided geograpically and labeled with the names of the modern Mexican states of Jalisco, Colima and Nayarit, within whose borders they are found, although they spilled over into Michoacán to the southeast and Sinaloa to the northwest. They have often and incorrectly been called Tarascan, after the people whose powerful empire spread throughout Michoacán during the Historic Period and who became such fierce enemies of the Aztecs. However, the Tarascans did not make their appearance in history until after these cultures disappeared.

The oldest figurine style found in Jalisco follows the "gingerbread" concept of the flat figurines of Chupícuaro, but on a somewhat larger scale, and with abstracted, stylized forms replacing the minute detail of the Chupícuaro figurines. The Jalisco figures most often represent dancers, standing on flexed legs, somewhat in the manner of a cowboy's stance, and with arms spread out. Other figurines show personages with tall, conical hats or headdresses, seated cross-legged in solemn posture. Sometimes they represent a woman with a baby at her breast; and in one marvelous variation, a woman is shown with a score of tiny baby figures crawling all over her mountainous form. Although these figurines are the most archaic type found in Jalisco, they apparently continued to be made after new and technically more advanced forms were developed. This is a characteristic demonstration of the unusual conservatism, the clinging to old established ways which was such a strong trait in all of the western village cultures and which must

have been a crucial factor in enabling them to survive for over a thousand years.

Another type of figure, found chiefly in and around the city of Guadalajara, was made of a coarse black clay completely covered with a finely polished red clay slip decorated with white designs and features. These small, solid figurines represent a people with a long-headed and long-nosed ideal of beauty which is curiously similar to that of the earliest, Preclassic figurines found at Teotihuacán. They are usually shown wearing turbanlike headdresses, and sometimes finely patterned skirts and shoulder capes, the women often with a baby, the men playing drums. Sometimes whole family groups are found in which the varying sizes of the figures seem to indicate the relative status and importance of each member.

Still later in the cycle of stylistic development are the large, hollow figures for which Jalisco is most famous. They include some of the great triumphs of the clay sculpture of the villages. Their beautifully modeled, powerful forms and impressive size are evidence of the expert assurance and sculptural daring of their creators. They include dramatic figures of ballplayers, and of warriors in full armor, swinging their clubs in captured motion. More common, however, are figures of heavy-set nude women reminiscent, in their simultaneously massive and sensuous form, of the sculpture of Gaston Lachaise. They are sometimes shown kneeling, or sitting with one arm lifted up in a theatrical hailing gesture. Others are presented standing, holding a baby or a bowl of the indented oval type which occurs so often in pre-Columbian Mexico. Their finely detailed faces express an enormous dignity, and they have large hands with carefully indicated nails. Their arms are generally rather foreshortened in a tradition carried over from earlier archaic stylizations. These are all hollow figures, conceived and executed fully in the round, usually between twelve and thirty inches high. Their surface was covered with a slip of fine creamy-white clay, or red, or both, side by side. The slip was burnished and decorative details such as facial decorations outlined with black paint applied with a very fine brush.

The most talented school of village sculptors developed in a
small region on the Pacific Coast in the shadow of the 13,000-foot-
high Colima volcano, which has lent its name to the modern state
as well as to the ancient art style. The earliest figures found here
are a local variation of the small votive female figurines typical of
the Preclassic horizon. Characteristic traits of these sand-colored
clay figurines include elegantly tapered, elongated legs which end
in fine points, herringbone-patterned body designs applied with
black paint and, unique in Mexico, detailed marking of sexual

characteristics. This ancient prototype form continued to be made long after more elaborate figurine forms had been developed. It was adapted to represent women engaged in every imaginable type of activity—women with children in their laps or on their breasts, women grinding corn and making tortillas, pregnant women, old women with sagging bosoms, sick or dead women on ceremonial pallets. There are also figurines of men, some nude, some elaborately dressed in warrior costumes with eagle feathers, helmets and huge, man-high rectangular curved shields. Others represent dancers, musicians playing drums, flutes, rattles and conch shell trumpets, chieftains seated in their palanquins and medicine men wearing masks. Sometimes whole groups of figurines were put together on a clay base, such as six boys and six girls holding one another's arms and dancing around a group of musicians. In the same style are small representations of animals—dogs, turkeys, frogs, armadillos and deer—usually with a whistle or a rattle buried inside them.

Colima sculptors discovered that the greatest practicable size for solid clay figurines was about twelve inches. Larger figurines just could not be fired satisfactorily in their simple ovens, for it is typical even of small solid figurines that the inner core is not fired all the way through. The logical next step was to make figurines the way bowls and vases were made—that is, hollow, and with air

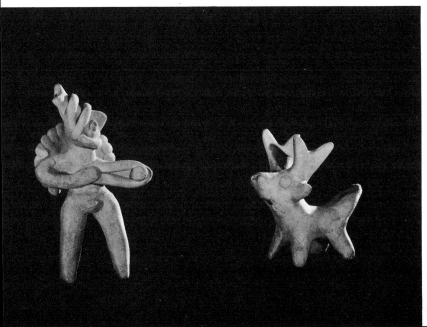

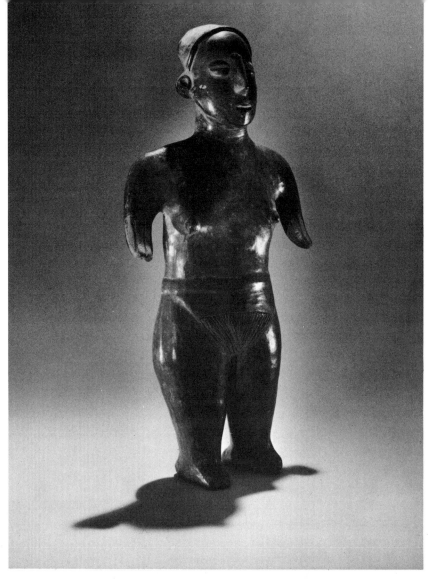

holes so that they would not explode during the firing process. But so conservative were these people that for a considerable transition period hollow figures were indeed made, but they followed the form and two-dimensional aesthetic of their gingerbread predecessors. Only very slowly, step by step, were these figures expanded into realistic, three-dimensional form. Technically, however, great improvements began to take place with the first hollow figures; the surface was burnished before firing, to produce a rich, deeply glowing sheen, and the "negative paint" technique of decoration began to be used. This consists of applying a color, usually black, on the light-brown or red surface of the figure or bowl in such a way that the design appears in red, or brown, on a black background. A similar technique is still used in the decoration of batik fabrics; it calls for the careful waxing of the areas of the design which are not to be painted, the wax being scraped off as soon as the color which is to represent the design's background has been applied.

The full flourishing of the Colima style produced masterpieces which are among the high points in pre-Columbian art. The sculptors of Colima brilliantly solved the technical problems inherent in clay, and they were able to transcend the limitations of their medium. As their figurines of men and plants and animals amply demonstrate, they were amazingly perceptive realists. More than that, they were able to translate their accurate observations of nature into forms with a sensuous, tactile surface that is equaled only in Olmec art.

These reddish-brown, beautifully burnished figures portray the whole panorama of their world, men and women, plants and animals, with extraordinary individual presence and grace. Parrots, pelicans, armadillos, turtles, snakes, snails, shells, fishes, coati mundis and dogs were portrayed with perceptive realism in clay effigies made to accompany the dead on the long road to the afterlife. Dogs were an important commodity among these votive food providers, as they were in real life, for this was a world without cattle or pigs or sheep, and its fattened dogs were its major supply

of meat. They were a special breed of dogs, the Mexican hairless, which disappeared but have been successfully bred back again in recent years. When not fattened they look somewhat like dachshunds, but with slightly longer legs. Their warm, wrinkled gray skin is the color of stone, which has given them their Indian name of *tepescuintl*, or *techichi* (*tetl*, "stone"; *chichi*, "dog"). One of the early Spanish missionaries, Fray Bernardino de Sahagún, mentions them as "the dogs of the country, totally without hair . . . short and round, delicious to eat."

Representations of pumpkins, gourds, squashes and edible cacti were usually made in the form of bowls which held food offerings. An especially lovely form occasionally found is that of a large pumpkin supported on three legs in the form of small parrots, which hold the vegetable with their beaks while their tails lightly touch the ground. Another variation shows the pumpkin supported by three small human figures, sometimes almost bent double under their heavy load, sometimes playfully and defiantly standing on tiptoe with feet crossed like a ballet dancer. The sides of other bowls are decorated with the high-relief forms of shrimp, crabs, fishes and dogs.

Their representations of men and women are the most varied and imaginative in pre-Columbian Mexico. They portrayed chieftains and dignitaries, servants and carriers with heavy loads on their backs and shoulders, musicians, acrobats, warriors, ballplayers, hunchbacks and dwarfs. Women are shown with babies, or pregnant, although they appear less often than they do in the

more archaic small figurines. Unique in Mexico are their representations of seated dwarfs with enormously exaggerated genitals, one of the very rare examples of erotica in Middle American art. But it is an interesting documentation of the realism of the clay sculptors of Colima that even here they are true to life, portraying a peculiarity of achondroplastic dwarfs: the combination of a diminutive body with genitals the same size as those of a normal man. This disproportion has been seen as a fertility symbol by many peoples around the world, including the ancient Egyptians, whose god Nu is shown as a dwarf with the same anatomical proportions.

The practical, realistic nature of the people of Colima is demonstrated also by their frequent combination of figures and bowls into effigy vessels. As figures had to be hollow for technical reasons in any case, many of them were provided with slightly enlarged air holes around which a small, collarlike neck was placed so that the figure could also serve as a vessel in the afterlife. A final triumph of technique permitted air holes so small that they could be placed in the eyes of the figure, which gives some Colima figures an extraordinary sense of mysterious presence.

The third region where the village cultures persisted is that covered by the state of Nayarit and the southern reaches of Sinaloa on the Pacific Coast. Two distinctly different, apparently successive styles developed here. The large, hollow figures of the earlier style are quite closely related to the fully developed figures of Colima; they have the same kind of patiently burnished, elegantly finished surface and the use of negative black paint decoration, although the Nayarit figures preserve many more archaic traits in their sculptural forms. Typical are its very tall representations of nude women with comparatively small heads and tiny arms, holding a miniature bowl on one shoulder or in front of the stomach. The large bosoms, long bodies, exaggerated legs and enormous feet give these figures a conical effect. Closely related are the figures of pregnant women seated or kneeling in the birth-giving position still used by many Indians, the hands pressing down on the large

abdomen. Men are sometimes shown as musicians, playing on percussion instruments made of turtle shells or on conch-shell trumpets. More often they are portrayed as warriors holding maces, wearing helmets and barrel-shaped armor made of basketry, the weave of which is indicated by the same kind of finely incised lines the sculptors of Nayarit used to indicate the carefully combed hair of their subjects. Curiously, this armor always stops just below the waist, as if a kind of Marquess of Queensberry rules was observed in their wars. Some of the most beautiful examples of the art of the fossilized village cultures are made in this style. Their often exaggerated, sometimes fantastic stylizations were always executed with an unerring sense of sculptural form.

The other figurine style is often called Ixtlán, after the site in southern Nayarit where it was first identified. Characteristic of the style are the rougher, often unburnished surfaces of its figures, which are embellished with brightly painted, polychrome decorations. Many are shown wearing elaborate mantles, skirts, shoulder capes and headdresses, whose material is faithfully reproduced in black, red, white and orange. Nayarit textiles seem to have been woven in geometric designs—diamonds, zigzags, stepped lines and stripes—which were broken up into individual squares or rectangles that repeated or alternated the different motifs. The same patterns were reproduced also on polychrome bowls, which often follow gourd and pumpkin forms.

The artists of Ixtlán, with their anecdotal realism, have given an extraordinary insight into their people's daily life and habits. They depicted all the members of their society, from small children at their mothers' breasts to old men and women bent with age and wasted by diseases whose symptoms are so clearly illustrated that physicians can easily identify them. A favorite subject was a marital couple sitting side by side, sometimes even sculpted as one double figure. The wife is usually shown nursing a child or holding a food bowl, while the husband has a musical instrument or a ceremonial fan. The artists often seem touchingly, somewhat naïvely preoccupied with such minute details as the exact number

of earrings worn by each individual. Unlike the other people of Middle America, the men and women of Nayarit did not wear ear plugs; they wore true earrings, one next to the other, through the ear lobe and on up the side of the ear, sometimes as many as a dozen at a time. The same kind of earring was worn also through the septum of the large, aquiline nose which was a proud trait of these villagers.

The climax of the anecdotal art of Nayarit is found in the lively, elaborate representations of their houses, ball courts and ceremonies. The documentary insight that they give us, into the daily life of these villages, is unique in ancient America. There are small, windowless round huts and large, well-built two-story houses with steep painted roofs, breezeways on the second floor, one or more stairways, and a generally windowless ground floor. These are almost always shown with all their inhabitants in the pursuit of their daily tasks, the women cooking or grinding corn and making tortillas, nursing babies, while lovers embrace and dogs and children play. There are representations of ceremonial ball courts, with a game in progress and the sloped sides of the court filled with masses of spectators. Other large group representations show funerals, religious ceremonies and the famous *volador* game still played in remote villages. This game calls for the erection of a tall pole, from which men, at the ends of long ropes fastened around their chests, jump and fly in imitation of birds. The game also had ritual significance, representing the course of the sun.

The art of Nayarit and the other western village cultures was long considered as little more than barbaric. Not many years ago, when such figures were accidentally found, ranchers used them as targets for Sunday shooting practice. But, beginning some thirty years ago, modern artists rediscovered the appealing, meaningful art of these ancient villages, and the first collections were formed, the most important of which was the famous collection of Diego Rivera. The realization that the old pots and figures which were found on their land were actually worth money soon stopped the willful destruction and caused entire villages to become full-

time tomb hunters and explorers. When nearby sources began to run dry for some of the gravediggers, they began to pay the ultimate compliment to their ancient predecessors by fabricating their works. Fortunately, the technical flaws and stylistic errors in even their best efforts render the forgeries easily detectable.

To the southeast of this region, along the Pacific Coast and within the present State of Guerrero, is one of the most interesting archaeological areas of Mexico, and, paradoxically, it is the least explored. According to the richly promising archaeological evidence discovered here, this region must have played an extremely important role during Preclassic and early Classic times.

The coast near Acapulco boasts a now partly submerged site of an elaborate archaic village culture which produced a distinct and lovely type of small clay female figurine with uniquely tall, elegantly detailed headdresses. They have close resemblances to the Preclassic figurines from the Valley of Mexico, but until now little has been published about them. Somewhat further inland from here, clay figurines of another style have been found, the most primitive in Mexico. They are crudely baked, immensely heavy figurines of coarse reddish clay which is almost always covered with a grayish-white slip, standing some nine to twelve inches high. They invariably represent women, who are shown standing in the bent-legged stance characteristic of Olmec figurines, the head tilted back somewhat as if gazing upward in adoration. Their arms are stylized in the abbreviated archaic convention. Their eyes and other details are indicated by methods typical of the earliest sculptors: small, straight-line incisions in the clay, and *pastillaje*, the adding of small round or elongated clay pellets to form the eyes, nose, breasts, ornaments and other details. The unique and most striking feature of these figurines is a deep, channellike incision which is found on all of them, running from the chestbone to the navel of their protruding, probably pregnant abdomens.

These figurines have a power, and at the same time a sense of brutality, that is staggering. Most people initially turn away from them with a slight shudder at their obsessive "ugliness," but the force of their sculptural form is as undeniable as it is insinuating. Once the censorship of the initial shock reaction is relaxed, they are easily recognized as among the most dramatic, vigorous examples of pre-Columbian art. One is reminded by them of some of the paintings of Dubuffet and what is called the *art brut* school of contemporary painting. The crucial difference is that once one has seen these clay figures from Guerrero most *art brut* looks tame in comparison, like a witty parlor game. One is made to feel that the sculptors of Guerrero worked with an absolute conviction to represent a brutal daily reality of their time.

No archaeological associations are known for these figures, and no excavations have yet been carried out where they have been found. It is known only that they are generally found in groups, interred in the earth in Indian file, one directly in front of the

other. A possible explanation is that they represent a variation of
the fertility ritual associated with all of the archaic votive female
figurines, and that this ritual involved a fearsome sacrificial rite,
as indicated by the long incision in the torso. This could be a later
local addition or possibly an ancient remnant long since given up
by the more advanced cultures of the highland valleys. Still to be
determined, possibly by Carbon-14 tests, is the question of whether
these figures represent one of the most ancient cultural levels in
Middle America or whether they are the product of an archaic-
culture pocket hidden in the rugged mountains of Guerrero, isolated from the main stream of civilization which developed in the
central highlands and on the Gulf Coast.

THE OLMECS

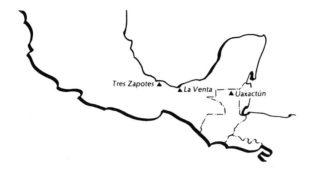

Tres Zapotes ▲　▲ La Venta ▲ Uaxactún

INTO THE WORLD OF THE FLOURISHING archaic villages a new culture suddenly intruded, and it was to have the most profound effects on the development of Indian civilization. Without leaving traces of earlier developmental stages that have been identified so far, a powerful, highly gifted people made their appearance in Mexico during the middle of the Preclassic Period. Indications of their widespread influence are first evident in superb figurines and objects of jade and other fine materials carved in a new, different and superbly accomplished style. These objects were interred at Tlatilco and elsewhere side by side with the bowls and figurines of the continuing village cultures.

The origin of these strange new people and their extraordinary culture is one of the most important of the still unsolved enigmas of American archaeology. Because of their apparent worship of the jaguar—whose features haunt their art so obsessively that it is often hard to decide whether a figure represents a man disguised as a jaguar or a jaguar assuming human form—this people and their culture are sometimes designated as "the jaguar people." For better or worse, however, they are more universally known by the basically irrelevant and inappropriate name Olmec, from the Aztecs' name for the "people from the lands of rubber."

The Aztecs of the fifteenth century of the Christian Era applied the name Olmec to a Gulf Coast people who had conquered the famous city of Cholula in the highland valley of Puebla and dominated it from about A.D. 800 to 1200. They are now referred to as the Historic Olmecs, but little is known of them and no decisive importance is attached to them. However, in the region of the Historic Olmecs' homeland on the Gulf Coast, important early temple-cities have been found whose magnificent monuments mark the apogee of the splendid, unmistakable style of the jaguar people. Thus it came about that the name Olmec was applied to this gifted Preclassic people, whose traces have been found all over Middle America and who developed the great mother culture from which the theocratic cultures of the later Classic Period derived so much of their spiritual and aesthetic inspiration.

Important Olmec centers have been found at sites known as La Venta, Tres Zapotes, Cerro de las Mesas and San Lorenzo, in Tabasco and southern Veracruz, the heart of the rubber country on the Gulf of Mexico. Extensive explorations and excavations have been carried out during the past twenty-five years at all of these ruined temple-cities, but the most important of them, and certainly the one that has yielded the richest and most instructive finds, is La Venta. Here, on an island surrounded by mangrove swamps, the Olmecs constructed a grand city of temples and pyramid-shaped temple platforms, with large ceremonial plazas for solemn assemblies and processions, colonnaded courts for priestly rituals, splendidly carved stone altars and enormous monumental stone slabs, or stelae, covered with fine bas-relief sculpture. The beginnings of the city go back as far as 1000 B.C., while the full development of its great architectural complex appears to have taken place between 800 B.C. and 300 B.C.

La Venta is the earliest known example of a temple-city of the type which flourished in many places all over Middle America

during the Classic Period. To understand the role of such a city, one might think of it as somewhat like Jerusalem in Old Testament times: a vital religious center to which a large part of the population of a considerable region repaired at stated intervals for great festivals and ceremonies. Secondarily, such cities also served as administrative centers for the priestly rulers who directed the fortunes of the temple-cities. But the minor role of administration, as opposed to the worship and glorification of the gods, is emphasized by the overwhelming predominance of religious structures and the paucity, if not total absence, of administrative buildings and residences. At La Venta all structural remnants are of a religious nature. It can be assumed that other buildings were not considered important enough to be constructed of stone. In the dense tropical rain-forest climate of Tabasco, no wooden structure can long survive without constant repairs.

The most extraordinary monuments at La Venta are a series of six colossal heads carved out of basalt, each measuring as much as nine feet in height and weighing some fifteen tons. The technical feat of their ancient sculptors and engineers is all the more astounding in view of the fact that they had to bring these heads, as well as all of the stone columns and stelae, from quarries more than sixty miles distant, through dense jungles and swamps to their island city. The massive stone heads portray men with characteristic Olmec features: thick, heavy lips, full cheeks, broad nostrils, almost swollen eyelids and a peculiar type of close-fitting headdress or helmet. Each of the heads is a complete sculpture in itself, and none appear to have been attached to a body.

An important precursor of later forms is the great stone stelae found at La Venta, erected and carved with elaborate bas-relief representations and calendric glyphs to commemorate great historic and astronomical events. Through careful observations carried on over the centuries, the Olmecs appear to have developed the first calendar and to have devised a system of calendric notation that produced the first forms of glyph writing. These crucial inventions formed part of the great legacy the Olmecs left to the

Classic Period—a legacy that was heavily drawn upon by the Maya and their contemporaries all over Middle America.

Other exciting finds at La Venta include huge monolithic stone altars. One of them has sculptured sides on which an Olmec priest is portrayed wearing an elaborate headdress and collar, sitting cross-legged and holding a child in his arms in an offertorial gesture. Another altar is decorated with dwarflike atlantean figures in bas-relief, all of which show the same typically Olmec facial characteristics found on the colossal heads. One of the most spectacular discoveries is a 15½-foot-square mosaic pavement of green serpentine slabs representing the highly stylized, geometric face of the jaguar god. Near this mosaic, an offertorial cache of six ax-blade-shaped jade celts and sixteen superb jade and serpentine figurines were uncovered in 1955. Happily, the entire find has been installed in the one museum in the exact position in which they were found: the fifteen jade figurines standing in a rough semicircle facing the single serpentine figure, and the flat jade celts arranged in the form of a palisade behind it. The meaning of the cache and the ritual it portrays are still obscure. The figurines, each of which is about eight inches in height, all show men standing in a characteristic Olmec stance, with flexed legs and loosely hanging arms, the head thrown slightly back, a position which brings to mind the stance of dancers as well as a state of religious trance. They represent the Olmec physical type of relatively short, squat and fleshy men with clean-shaven, elongated, almost pear-shaped heads, a deformation deliberately effected by binding the head in infancy. Their short noses have perforations in the septum indicating the wearing of nose ornaments. Other typical Olmec traits shown in these figurines are fleshy necks, heavy jowls, stubborn chins and decidedly mongoloid eyes with puffed eyelids. The most important characteristic, however, is the mouth, drawn down at the corners like that of a crying baby and often emphasizing a thick, flaring upper lip that suggests the fierce mouth of a jaguar.

Since the jaguar was the great deity of the Olmecs, they felt a deep, mystic identification with this silent, powerful king of the

jungle. To him they dedicated their splendid art and ritual. The identification of men with animals was a basic concept of Indian thought and belief all through pre-Columbian times. It was held that human life was magically united in fate with that of the animal which is the *nahual*, or alter ego, of an individual as well as of an entire nation. These animals themselves were deified because they were also the earthly disguise of gods, because the gods too had *nahuals* in the form of animals in which they became incarnate.

Although the jaguar deity played the dominant role among the Olmecs, there is evidence also of an important duck-billed bird deity who is represented by the priest wearing a duck-billed disguise in the famous "Tuxtla Statuette" in the United States National Museum in Washington. The glyphs carved on this figurine spell out a date that has been variously interpreted as either 97 B.C. or A.D. 162. Later cultures adopted as their chief totemic animal the mythical bird-and-serpent combination, the plumed serpent Quetzalcóatl, which dominates the Classic Period, and the eagle, which represents the sun, during the Historic Period. The jaguar,

however, continued to play an important role in the pantheon of later times, being identified chiefly with the powers of the earth and its interior. In a brilliant, stylistic study, Miguel Covarrubias has shown how the Olmec jaguar mask was the prototype from which evolved, over a period of many centuries, the masks of the various rain gods of the later Maya, Zapotec and Teotihuacán cultures of Classic times.

Some of the finest of the half-jaguar, half-human Olmec faces are found on the great votive stone axes that were carved of jade and other hard stones. The finest of them, like the superb ax in the American Museum of Natural History, in New York, have such powerful sculptural forms and are carved with such absolute mastery over the hard material that they loom many times larger than one would be led to expect from their measurements, which rarely exceed one foot. The exact meaning of the large Olmec axes is still obscure, but they appear to be associated with thunder and lightning and thus with rain. The neolithic cultures of Asia and Europe associated stone axes with thunderbolts, and in Maya mythology it is related that the gods produced lightning by throwing large stone axes.

The Olmec sculptors handled the hardest of stones, and particularly jade, with unequaled skill and imposed their forms with surprising sureness and perfection of technique. No evolutionary steps in the development of this art can be traced; it seems to have sprung forth full-blown. The forms they gave their objects and figures have great refinement and a deceptive simplicity. Their sensuously modeled and polished surfaces are often relieved by typical incisions of fine, sharply traced lines. These serve to highlight details of the figures and frequently depict stylized Olmec profiles that appear again and again as decorative and probably magic elements on the surfaces of jade objects. Unlike the lapidaries of succeeding cultures whose forms and style were limited by the hardness of stone and by the mechanical methods employed, the Olmecs completely dominated their materials. Their jades have the same strong, flowing forms and powerful, realistic representa-

tions that are found in their clay figures; in fact, the distinctive Olmec style is apparent no matter what material they used. In carving jade, the Olmecs appear to have employed all the methods known to later times: cutting the stone with a string, abrading it, crumbling by percussion, drilling with bone and stone drills, and polishing with finely powdered hard materials.

To the Olmecs and all later cultures, jade was the most valuable of all substances. It was the symbol of everything precious and divine in this world, perhaps because it is of the color of water and vegetation. Even after the introduction of gold and silver into Mexico about the tenth century, jade continued to be prized much more highly than precious metals. A dramatic illustration of this is recorded in the chronicle of Bernal Díaz del Castillo, one of Cortes's soldiers who participated in the conquest of the Aztec capital of Tenochtitlán. When the Aztecs forced the first Spanish invaders to flee for their lives during the famous *Noche Triste*, many of the greedy newcomers among the Spanish soldiery were drowned while crossing the water, loaded down by their heavy loot of gold. The experienced old soldier, however, saved his life and his fortune by pocketing a few jade beads, which he knew the Indians valued much more highly than gold.

For many years it was doubted that jade was found in Middle America, because no deposits had been traced in modern times, and there was much speculation about the origin of pre-Columbian jade and its possible sources and importation. However, jade occurs only rarely in veins or large deposits; it generally appears in isolated boulders in ravines and river beds. The secret of finding jade, as well as the art of carving it, was one of the gifts of the Olmecs to the later cultures. How their jade hunters searched for the precious material was first described by the Franciscan missionary of early Conquest days, Fray Bernardino de Sahagún. Convinced that it was necessary to understand fully the Indians' beliefs and history before he could successfully convert them to Christianity, this imaginative friar taught a group of young men from noble Aztec families how to use the Roman alphabet to write their own language and then sent them out to interview all the surviving Indian officials, priests and sages they could find. From them was collected all they knew about the physical and spiritual life of their people, their legends, beliefs, religion, customs, traditions and history. Sahagún's great work, *Historia general de las cosas de Nueva España* ("General History of the Things of New Spain"), is the first exact, factual report in history based on objective observations of a strange people, prepared fully in accordance with modern anthropological techniques. Concerning jade, Sahagún's Aztec informants recalled:

> There are those who know where precious stones grow, and in fact a precious stone, wherever it is, emanates a subtle vapor or steam, and said vapor arises at sunrise and at sunset, and those who search for such stones place themselves in a convenient place at sunrise and look in the direction of the sun, and when they see the delicate smoke rising, they know there are precious stones there, which have been born or were hidden in that place. They go to that place, and if they find a stone from which the vapor came they know it contains a precious stone and they break it to find it.

An interesting sidelight is that in China professional jade prospectors also searched for jade in deep, remote ravines and maintained as jealously guarded family secrets their methods of identifying jade-bearing boulders. The Chinese and the ancient Indians also observed the custom of placing a small object or bead of jade in the mouth of the dead, and of painting funerary jade offerings red.

The Olmec lapidaries preferred a translucent, blue-green type of jade, although they also used spinach-colored jade and pale-green to white jade. Emerald-green jade does not appear until considerably later, when it was used chiefly by the Maya of the Classic Period. The Olmecs carved a surprising variety of objects out of jade, generally using fine blue-green jade of the most beautiful among them. There are round disks with human and jaguar masks

engraved with fine incised lines, round and cylindrical beads and an infinite variety of gorgets and pendants in the form of stylized clam shells, jaguar teeth, human hands, toes, legs, ears, stingray tails and deer jaws, and others of abstracted forms no longer readily identifiable. One of the most beautiful Olmec jade objects known is a hollowed-out canoe, which when turned upside down is a magnificently simplified human hand.

Among the most prized jade objects are masks and complete human figurines of the type found in the offertorial cache at La Venta. These range in size from as small as one inch up to more than ten inches; but of the larger figures only the broken heads have generally survived. These masks and figures represent two distinct variations of the Olmec physical type. One has a broad, flat nose and heavy lips, similar to the colossal heads found at La Venta, although the crying-baby or jaguar aspect of the mouth is often more heavily emphasized. The other type is distinguished by a thin, high-bridged aquiline nose and relatively thin lips. The two types are easily recognized, but their implication is one of the many fascinating aspects of Olmec culture that await full exploration and study.

The same mastery which the Olmecs displayed in their carving of jade is found in their stone sculpture. In a figure such as the famous basalt sculpture of a seated wrestler (exhibited in the Museo Nacional in Mexico City), an unknown Olmec genius reached heights of lifelike expressiveness and sculptural drama which were not to be equaled until the great renaissance of stone sculpture under the Aztecs during the second half of the fifteenth century. Their stone carvers excelled in all they touched. They left us magnificent stone sarcophagi, unique in Middle America, towering stone stelae and massive altars with splendid scenes represented in low relief and grandiose conceptions carved on great rock walls in caves and on mountainsides.

Although the Olmecs were stone sculptors par excellence, they carried over into their modeling of clay the same masterful sensitivity, though pottery was a distinctly minor technique for them. A typical Olmec method was to wait until the clay was almost dry before carving it, giving their pottery a characteristically dramatic quality. Olmec clay and stone vessels have a distinctive flat-bottomed, straight-sided profile, different from the rounded forms created by the village potters, and it seems to have provided a better surface for incised decorations and designs.

The Olmecs may also have been the discoverers of the art of making hollow clay figures, thus making possible the firing of larger figures. The relatively low temperatures obtainable in ancient firing ovens rendered it difficult and impractical to make solid figures more than twelve inches tall. Even the smaller solid figurines rarely were fired all the way through, as can clearly be seen when they are broken. Hollow figurines are technically harder to build, and they pose additional problems in firing, but the Olmecs solved all of these technical problems and produced clay figures executed fully in the round, of an unprecedented and never-again-equaled sculptural quality. The most beautiful Olmec clay figurines have been found at Tlatilco, covered with a fine slip of burnished white kaolin. Some represent men seated in a Buddha-like position, infinitely distinguished even though portrayed

without any clothing. Others, of a type known as "Baby Face," represent chubby children with the typical flared mouth of the Olmecs, sitting on the ground with their legs spread like a small infant's, hands resting on their knees.

There are few representations of women in Olmec art, and the few that do occur are generally small clay figurines more closely related to the archaic female figurines of the village cultures than to the monumental art of La Venta. Very possibly they represent a kind of compromise or crossing between the two cultures, between the simple, direct art of the female fertility cult of the early villages and the male-oriented art of the Olmec priests.

In recent years Olmec objects have been found all over Middle America. One of the most beautiful Olmec jades, representing a bat deity, was found in Costa Rica. Olmec rock carvings exist in the Valley of Morelos near Cuernavaca, in Guatemala and even as far as El Salvador. The influence of the style can be clearly recognized in figurines made as far away as the Ohio Valley. Miraculously, even a wooden object carved in the purest Olmec style has survived in the famous life-size inlaid wooden mask in the American Museum of Natural History, in New York; it was found in a dry cave near Taxco in the State of Guerrero. As noted earlier, rich finds of Olmec objects and figurines have been excavated at Tlatilco and also at Tlapacoya in the Valley of Mexico, where they are found mixed with objects made in the earlier local traditions. Olmec-style objects have been found in the great acropolis of Monte Albán in Oaxaca, whose early monuments bear witness to very strong Olmec influences. The most important of these are the famous *Danzantes*—large stone slabs with incised designs—that decorate the earliest temple of Monte Albán. They depict strange, dwarflike personages in positions reminiscent of dancers (hence their name), drawn in loose, fluid lines an inch or so wide, carefully pecked out of the smooth surface of the flat stone. They are Olmec in spirit and detail, and on one group of slabs, presumably later than the others, glyph writing and the bar-and-dot numerical systems that continued to be used until the Conquest make their first appearance.

Another significant monument built in a style heavily dominated by Olmec motifs was uncovered in the great Classic Maya
city of Uaxactún, on the border between Mexico and Guatemala.
There, archaeologists found a breathtakingly beautiful, completely intact early pyramid decorated with masks of the jaguar
god of the Olmec; it was hidden inside a later Classic Maya pyramid that covered it like a tent. It is a pattern of construction found
at many other sites, where pyramids were periodically enlarged
by superimposing new, larger structures over earlier, smaller ones.

Some pyramids that have been explored are like Russian toy Easter eggs, one hidden inside another hiding still another yet smaller one, and so on, up to as many as six layers. The pyramid at Uaxactún is known by the unimaginative name "E-VII-Sub," because it was located inside the seventh pyramid of a group of pyramids labeled "E" on the first maps of the site. Although only twenty-seven feet high, the pyramid is ascended on all four sides by huge ceremonial staircases which are flanked by rows of jaguar-god masks of creamy-white stucco, each some six feet high and eight feet wide.

The list of extraordinary Olmec finds grows almost year by year. It is likely that other, still unexplored ruins in the dense jungle of southern Mexico and Guatemala will continue to yield new treasures. The relatively unexplored regions of Guerrero and the coast of Oaxaca should also provide important clues and pieces with which to complete the unfinished jigsaw puzzle of this great mother culture of Middle America. Despite our limited knowledge of the Olmecs, there can be little doubt that they were the progenitors of the theocratic cultures of the Classic age.

Where did the Olmecs come from? Where did they go through their formative stages? What is the meaning of their curious similarity to the powerful early Chavin culture in Peru, or the haunting Oriental feeling evident in many Olmec objects? The problem has been outlined and explored at length by Miguel Covarrubias and the Mexican archaeologist Wigberto Jiménez Moreno. Covarrubias's tentative history, which was published posthumously in 1957, still appears to be the most likely, and recent discoveries have repeatedly given support to his theories.

The earliest Olmec objects are, very possibly, certain rudimentary stone figurines which possess decided Olmec characteristics but are carved with only the simplest, massive shapes and geometric incisions. An interesting example of this early style is now exhibited in the Covarrubias collection in the Museo Nacional, in Mexico City. There is also a striking correspondence with the earliest clay figurines found in Guatemala, of the types known as Las Charcas and Mamóm. However, because the most archaic Olmec forms appear in Guerrero and Oaxaca, Covarrubias suggested that the origins of Olmec culture may one day be found along the coast and in the valleys of these two Pacific Coast states. The cult of stone axes and the distinctive Olmec trait of making stone vessels both appear to date from this period, which can probably be dated at the same time as the earliest agricultural people in the Valley of Mexico, probably about 2000 B.C.

It would seem, therefore, that the culture of the Olmecs might have spread from an area near the Pacific Coast northeast into the Valley of Mexico and into Veracruz and Tabasco, where a grand climax was reached at La Venta and Tres Zapotes, and that its influence radiated into the lowland Maya region. During the period of its geographical diffusion, Olmec art underwent growing elaboration and refinement. Typical is the development of finely incised

lines on stone objects to depict symbolic motifs and glyphs, and rapid, brilliant advances in jade carving. The splendid clay figurines and jade objects of Tlatilco belong to this period. The ultimate triumph of Olmec art was reached in the masterful tackling of monumental sculpture in the temple-cities on the Gulf Coast: the great basalt altars, stelae, sarcophagi and colossal heads. This latter period can probably be placed between 1000 B.C. and 500 B.C.

The third and final period saw the beginning of a stylistic decadence. The more rigid later forms, frozen by ritual prescription, began to be transformed and incorporated into the styles of the various rapidly developing local Classic cultures in such cities as Monte Albán and Uaxactún. At the same time the Olmecs appear to have been increasingly pressed on all sides by new people reaching ascendancy, in large part through the very hierocratic social system that they had learned from the Olmecs. La Venta probably was the last redoubt of the once great and powerful Olmec rulers. There is certainly clear enough evidence of its final violent collapse and the death of Olmec culture in the deliberate destruction of monuments at La Venta. Significantly, only Olmec faces were smashed on the altars and stelae, while faces with other physical characteristics were left intact. This would support the theory that the final overthrow of the Olmecs must have been accomplished by a foreign people, possibly the nearby Maya.

In looking back over the course of Olmec development, one sees as its most striking feature the tremendous degree of social organization which must have been required to enable them to plan and complete their elaborate, extensive temple-cities, works that must have involved the co-ordinated activity of thousands of workmen over long periods of time. In an age when the rest of Middle America still lived only in small, independent communities of farmers and fishermen, these were stupendous achievements indeed. It could have been accomplished only by a devoted elite of powerful, intelligent hierarchs. It is likely that they were the sages who, through generations of careful observation of the firmament, plotted the first calendar and pondered the nature of the gods who, by giving and withholding the blessings of the seasons, the rains and the essential crops of corn, directed man's fate. Priests planned the great propitiatory ceremonies and sacrifices which would appease the angry natures of the gods; and they erected temples on mounds and pyramids which represented the mountaintop abodes of the gods. In honor of heavenly climaxes such as solstices and eclipses they erected stelae, while on other commemorative stones they recorded the Olmec's earthly victories and the great events of state. Impressive public ceremonies must have taken place on the beautifully planned plazas in front of the important temples, and other, secret ones in the small temple sanctuaries in front of the idols of the gods themselves.

Even though the Olmecs were overthrown and destroyed—ironically, by some of the very peasant peoples to whom they had first brought the benefits of high civilization—their gifts, their inventions and their spirit lived on for a thousand years through all of the Classic Period and even beyond, until the Spanish Conquest. The awe in which they were held by later peoples is evident in the Olmec objects that were treasured and traded for centuries thereafter. Broken Olmec jades were kept as amulets, and these have often been found with later perforations that permitted their being restrung and worn again. Though the Olmecs were, like the ancient Greeks, destroyed, later generations continued to follow in the footsteps of their great priests, artists and astronomers, and their heritage remained alive.

MEZCALA

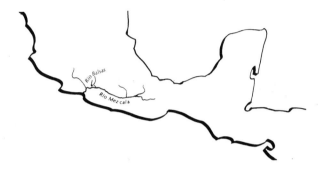

AMONG THE MOST IMPORTANT and characteristic Olmec traits are the cult of votive stone celts and the unique development of anthropomorphic stone axes. It is one of the oldest aspects of Olmec culture, and if, as Covarrubias suggested, the early stages of Olmec art are to be found in Guerrero, there is a special and closely related significance to the celt-based votive stone figurines of the early culture of Mezcala. Only recently has the study of this culture begun.

Mezcala figurines and masks are found in a well-defined area in the central part of the state of Guerrero, along the reaches of the Rio Mezcala and its tributaries, which later form the great Balsas river. This is the same area in which the great bulk of what can best be defined as "primitive Olmec" figurines has been found, the simple, quite rudimentary and probably very early versions of the type of figurines discovered in such splendid perfection at La Venta. The art of Mezcala seems to have sprung from the same soil and out of the same profound mythical involvement with the magic meaning of stone celts.

The typical Mezcala figure appears to have been carved out of a stone celt. Many figurines are, in fact, halfway between a celt and a fully defined figure, although in others the only reminder of the original celt form and meaning is found in the purposely roughened or unfinished surface on the top of the head, which looks as if it were made to be the receiving end of a chisel. In most standing figurines the legs are tapered until they come to a knifelike edge where the figure's feet would be. The division between the legs is a sharp and usually unpolished cut, while in some small figurines the legs are not separated at all, emphasizing even more strongly their basic celt form. Like Olmec figurines, Mezcala celt figures almost always represent men; only a small minority represent women, sometimes a pregnant woman, and sometimes a woman with a child on her back or at her side.

A possible explanation of the function and stylistic development of Mezcala sculpture may be contained in the famous offertorial cache of La Venta. Here sixteen Olmec figurines and six celts were found arranged in a circle, standing as if in the middle of a ritual ceremony. Another key may be provided by the large quantities of relatively simply carved, unpolished and poorly executed Mezcala stone figurines which have been found, such as the huge lot that was assembled and photographed by the archaeologist Gordon F. Ekholm on the banks of the Mezcala river.

They would seem to indicate that a wide, popular expansion of the votive celt and stone celt figurine took place in Guerrero, probably springing from the same sources as the Olmec celt cult. At the same time, the flourishing cult created an unprecedented demand for stone figurines and made the development of mass-production techniques imperative. Faced with the growing ritual demand for more and more celt figurines, the Mezcala sculptors developed a powerful, expressive style of abstraction remarkably close to that of many twentieth-century artists. Different figures bring to mind, in turn, Brancusi, Klee, Flanagan, and Henry Moore, as well as the cubists. The important difference is one of motivation—modern artists were engaged in a search for essential forms impelled by

visual and aesthetic curiosity, while Mezcala sculptors were driven by sheer physical necessity. Forced to work hard stone with only the simplest tools, and required to produce immense quantities of figures for their rituals, they had to find simplifications and stylizations so that the fewest lines and the most economical forms would express all the essential features of the human body. To appreciate the full force of their motivation, one must remember the underlying conviction of all ancient Indian religions: that only through perpetual, unceasing propitiation could the gods of nature be controlled, the vital corn crop be assured, and mankind be spared the visitations of floods and droughts and famine.

The very "modern," abstract quality which is so appealing today in Mezcala sculpture stood in the way of its recognition until very recently. It was considered too crude, too simple, to be of much aesthetic or archaeological interest. Nothing more than occasional, brief passing references were published on the culture until the publication, in 1956, of Covarrubias's small book, in which he defined the culture and in which he and this author first gave the culture its name. Until then, it had been grouped with the various other cultures found in this state and catalogued under the label Guerrero. Significantly, Mezcala art began to be appreciated and collected during the 1930s and '40s, by artists among whom were Diego Rivera, Henry Moore, André Breton, Herbert Ferber and Jacques Lipchitz. Its forms appeared to be so modern in concept that some prominent European archaeologists at first seriously questioned the authenticity of all Mezcala figures.

The American Museum of National History, in New York, has owned some two hundred Mezcala figurines since 1897, when it acquired the collection of William Niven. He appears to have been the first archaeological explorer of this region; in 1894, and again in 1896, he made extensive explorations of the Mezcala region of Guerrero, making many small excavations and bringing back a huge collection of pre-Columbian material. But so little attention has been paid to the art of this region since then that Niven's fascinating diary to this day remains unpublished, and it is virtually unknown in the archives of the museum. The excerpts below explain something of the difficulties which helped to discourage archaeologists from investigating this region, and they give a first-hand insight into the heroic problems which beset the early explorers.

August 19, 1896. Arrived at Ahuehuepan, an Indian town about 12 miles from the Mezcala River, near the summit of a rough and broken ridge. We purchased a number of small idols and a green diorite mask. The town is built on the steep sides of a barranca. Took a picture of some huts and church. We pitched our tent near the place, and at night Indian natives, men, women and children, at least 300 of them, formed in procession. Each carried a lighted candle, and the crowd was led by eight stalwart peons bearing shoulder-high a life-sized wooden figure of the Virgin Mary. Round and round the plaza they marched until nearly midnight, singing and shouting out their prayers and wildly imploring Almighty God to save their crops by sending them rain. The clanging of the bells, the beating of the drums, the shrieks of the marchers and the firing and glare of rockets made a scene of excitement and pandemonium for which I cannot find a fitting simile. In the following morning I heard from my servant that our visit had not been regarded with favor by the chief, who declared that the objects we were in search of were highly treasured by the Indians themselves, believing as did their forefathers, that they were Gods of Air. The chief commanded the Indians to refuse any assistance in digging the mounds which were to be found all over the neighborhood. He also expressed the opinion that we were probably spies and would inform the Mexican government regarding the procession we had witnessed and which had taken place contrary to law. Our reply to the chief was that his suspicions were unfounded, that our visit was a friendly one and that our only interest in the antiquities was of a scientific character. As the Indians had refused even to sell us corn, we decided to leave this inhospitable town, and procuring a guide, we were soon on the trail for Xochipala, where we arrived on the next day. Here we were received very kindly by the chief. After securing our former guide we started out early on the following morning for the ruins. The first indications of the prehistoric habitations were observed about half a day's journey west of the town.

August 22, 1896. At the beginning, there were merely foundations, but as we neared the summit we discovered walls, three to four feet high and about two feet thick, of a building which measured from 40 to 100 feet square. On arriving at the top of the hill, we pitched our tent in a great temple with clearly defined walls 300 by 200 feet. In the center was an altar of solid masonry fifteen feet square at the base.

August 23, 1896. We camped at another temple and took several interesting photographs. A trench was dug, and in one of the altars we found a plaster wall, and on the plaster floor an abundance of beads and broken pottery, and also a number of masks, and a remarkable object of green diorite or jade with a cross on the back. . . .

The mass-produced figurines commonly found at Mezcala are simply and even cursorily carved out of rather plain, unpolished gray stone, with only the most essential features indicated on the figure. For exceptional figures, however, intended perhaps for the use of notables and priests, fine hard green stones such as metadiorites were used. On these the Mezcala sculptors lavished the greatest care, carving the unyielding stone with sureness and extraordinary sculptural sensitivity, and patiently working and rubbing the smoothly finished surfaces to a gleaming polish. These figures, the masterpieces of Mezcala art, are imbued with a monumentality that belies their always relatively small size, which ranges from as small as a couple of inches to rarely taller than fourteen inches.

The style developed in making celt-shaped figurines was applied to a large variety of other images. Most important among them are the stone masks, which range from tiny pendants, as small as one inch long, up to life size. Along with the celt figurines they fall into a number of stylistic subcategories that are easily recognized but still await archaeological classification. Some are distinguished by deeply incised, negative diagonal lines that indicate arms and cheeks while others show cheeks and eyebrows as small, rounded protrusions in the stone. Still others indicate only the mouth and eyes, or mouth and eyebrows, suggesting the rest of the face with a sharply edged protrusion of the nose formed by the meeting of the two planes which represent the cheeks, while those of still another type indicate eyes and mouth with shallow indentations and present a huge, aquiline nose. Some achieve marvelous visual suggestions through the use of sharply incised, gashlike lines, while others are carved more realistically in the round. In some, the Olmec heritage can still be seen in the flexed-knee stance of the legs, the head tilted back as if in adoration and arms held in an offertorial position, while a characteristically Olmec square incision decorates the back. Later Mezcala figures mirror new influences, as in the wide-band headdresses typical of the culture of Teotihuacán.

Small masks usually have one or two small drilled perforations through which they could be strung, to be worn ceremonially or as amulets; the large masks probably were used in funeral ceremonies. The repertory of Mezcala sculptors included also a wide range of animal figures, such as monkeys, squirrels, fish, birds, dogs, deer, snakes and turtles. Other frequently found forms include stone hands, miniature stone vessels, and small votive temple models. No ceremonial centers or temple pyramids have so far been explored in the region, but the many temple models indicate that the people of Mezcala were active architects. One temple model clearly shows a peaked thatched roof, but the majority obviously represent beam-and-lintel architecture, either in stone or in wood, with the temples often mounted on fairly high pedestals ascended by a central stairway. They range from two to five col-

umns in width; and some small models have been found with two and even three superimposed stories. Some show a human effigy standing between the central pillars, while others have a figure laid out horizontally across the roof, possibly representing a funeral ceremony.

A favorite theme of Mezcala sculptors was the portrayal of figures seated back to back, both men and animals. This has a certain curious parallel in Oceanic art. Another subject which brought out some of their most dramatic stylizations is squatting men, hands clasping their knees, and the head thrown back in a worshiping gesture. On these, as on almost all of the small animal figures, there is a small perforation near the bottom, probably for the purpose of tying the figures onto objects of religious or magic significance, which then were offered to the gods and interred in the earth. In the Covarrubias collection in the Museo Nacional, in Mexico City, there are two tiny human figurines still tied together and wrapped in the cloth in which they were buried.

At this time virtually nothing is known of the history of the people of Mezcala. There are, however, some revealing leads on the development of their art. Their celt figurines would indicate that they stemmed from the same roots from which many Mexican archaeologists believe the Olmecs came—the still unexplored regions of Guerrero and western Oaxaca, on the Pacific slope of Mexico. Unlike the Olmec elite, the people of Mezcala did not spread out from there into the Valley of Mexico and across to the Gulf Coast. Thus they shared with the Olmecs their original, basically stone-centered culture (no ceramics have yet been found in association with Mezcala figurines) and the ancient votive celt cult. But they were never exposed to the worship of the jaguar, which the Olmecs encountered in the tropical lowlands of the Gulf Coast. Instead, isolated in their rugged, remote mountain valleys, the people of Mezcala continued to pursue the cult of votive anthropomorphic celts and to develop a unique art style that flourished until it was slowly transformed and absorbed by the influences radiating from Teotihuacán. On a stylistic basis, therefore, it is possible to date Mezcala art with some confidence between 500 B.C. and A.D. 400.

THE FORMATIVE AGE

Cuicuilco▲ ▲Cholula

▲ Monte Albán

Triggered perhaps by the powerful influence of the Olmecs, a profound change began to occur in the village society that flourished in the highland valleys during the second half of the last millennium B.C. The villagers started to break the old molds of tribal life and with enormous energy managed to lift the level of their original simple farming culture to that of a great urban civilization. This did not happen everywhere at the same time but began very early making rapid progress in some places while little pockets of resistance continued, sometimes for centuries, in the old ways.

The spread of advanced agricultural techniques such as terracing and irrigation created a surplus of food and made it possible for some men to lift their heads from the tyranny of daily tasks to develop their special talents. The old shamans became full-time priests who could devote all of their time to the pursuit of ritual and the contemplation of the stars and the gods; highly skilled, specialized craftsmen brought new refinements and elaboration to the arts; traders began to bring rare and precious goods from distant places. Thus began the division of labor and the organization of society into classes.

The most dramatic evidence of this change is found in the beginnings of ceremonial architecture and the building of the great formal temple-cities that became the most characteristic trait of Middle American civilization and the focus for the expression of its energy and genius. The oldest of these in the Valley of Mexico has been found at Cuicuilco, just off the highway to Cuernavaca, outside Mexico City—close to where the shining new buildings of the University of Mexico now rise on the old lava bed called the Pedregal. Cuicuilco's great, round, stepped pyramid, clearly visible from the highway, is surrounded by new excavations, which have shown clear evidence of the beginning of urban development radiating from the religious center. Carbon-14 tests indicate that Cuicuilco was inhabited as early as 450 B.C., when its first earthen mound was built as a temple base. It was abandoned and its ruins were

flooded—and preserved—by a devastating lava flow that occurred about 100 B.C. At that time there was renewed activity of the volcanoes on the edge of the valley, and a stupendous eruption of the now extinct volcano Xitlé caused a large part of the valley to be abandoned, the surviving inhabitants fleeing to the eastern and northern shores of the great central lake. The smoking volcano and the terrifying, devastating catastrophe which it produced probably were the origin of the intensive, widespread worship of the first of the Indian gods of whom we have representations, the Fire God. He was generally represented as an old man with a heavily wrinkled face, seated cross-legged, and supporting on his head and shoulders a brazier in which fire offerings were made. The Fire God remained an important member of the pantheon until Aztec times, when he was appropriately known as the Old God, Huehuetéotl, and was still represented as an old man seated on the ground and supporting a brazier.

Another important site of this period has been found at Tlapacoya, situated on what was the eastern shore of the great lake which filled the center of the southern end of the Valley of Mexico. Recent large finds of figurines at Tlapacoya show close parallels with the style of Tlatilco, and perhaps an even stronger Olmec influence is visible in many of the clay figurines. Unfortunately, the ceramists of Tlapacoya had much poorer clay to work with; most of their figurines are made of a rather drab, grayish-brown clay. Further, both the white slip that covered them originally and the red paint used to highlight decorations and details were imperma-

nent, and generally only faint traces can be seen on the figurines that have been excavated to date.

The name given to this general period by archaeologists is Ticomán, after the site where objects of the dominant style of this time were first found. Along with representations of the Fire God —almost always carved of porous volcanic stone—typical expressions of Ticomán art are intricately incised, flat clay cylinders, from one to one and a half inches in diameter; these were used as earplugs, adornments inserted into the lobe of the ear, which was perforated in childhood, then gradually became distended. This type of adornment was used by most of the Middle American peoples, and enormously elaborate variations were often depicted in later representations of important priests and personages, especially during the Classic Period. To increase the size of the ornament, its outer surface, like an exaggerated flange on a railroad wheel, was made much larger than the inner part which fitted the ear lobe. Another elaboration, which was developed later, was the wearing of long ear rods that went through the center hole of the earplug and often reached down as far as the shoulders of the wearer. Clay earplugs were a specialty of the Ticomán period; later cultures used chiefly green stones and jade and, after the introduction of metallurgy, gold and silver.

Very early temple-city sites have been found in many parts of Middle America outside the Valley of Mexico. Among the more important explored centers are Monte Albán in Oaxaca, Montenegro in the mountains of the Mixteca, Cholula in the highland valley of Puebla, and El Opeño in Michoacán in western Mexico. The great Olmec centers on the Gulf Coast belong to this period, as do the early Maya sites of the Chicanel period. Recent discoveries have revealed that an amazingly highly developed, extremely advanced early Maya culture was already flourishing in the Guatemala highlands during this epoch. Future explorations in this region are likely to throw important new light on this still very incompletely understood formative period that led to the great theocratic regional cultures of the Classic Period.

TEOTIHUACAN

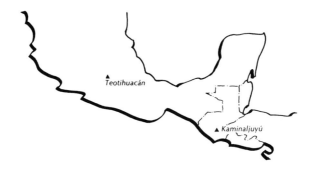

THE FIRST, THE LARGEST AND THE MOST grandiose manifestation of the new age of theocracies was the great city that rose to the northeast of the central lake in the Valley of Mexico, on a site which is still called by the name the Aztecs gave it, Teotihuacán ("Place of the Gods"). The city was already long abandoned and forgotten when the Aztecs arrived in the valley, but so impressive were its ruins that they believed the city had been built not by men but by the legendary *quinametin*, the giants who inhabited the earth before man arrived, and whose existence was documented for them by what they thought were human bones but were actually the skeletal remains of extinct prehistoric mammoths. The legend was believed even by the early conquistadors, who sent one such bone to the Emperor Charles V. It has also been suggested that the Aztecs' concept of the *quinametin* included not only physical but also intellectual dimensions, that they thought of the builders of these gigantic monuments as sages and creators of a golden age, somewhat as medieval Europeans thought of the ancients of Greece and Rome. Fray Bernardino de Sahagún quotes his informants on the subject, saying, ". . . they called the place Teotihuacán, burial place of kings; the ancients said: He who has died became a god; or when someone said—he who has become a god, meant to say—he has died. . . ."

Even today, thirteen centuries after its violent destruction, Teotihuacán is an awesome sight, a great dead city that spreads over more than six square miles, centered on two gigantic pyramids known (probably erroneously) as the Pyramid of the Sun and the Pyramid of the Moon. Around them, admirably planned and laid out, are the ruins of countless temples and palaces connected and interspaced by great avenues and ceremonial plazas. Once they were covered with gleaming layers of white and red stucco, although today most of the city appears as unexcavated rounded mounds overgrown with grass and bushes. Only a small percentage of its buildings have so far been uncovered, even though for sixty years it has been the most extensively studied archaeological site in Mexico.

The great Pyramid of the Sun stands some 210 feet high, and its base measures just under 700 feet square. Unlike many other pyramids, it was not constructed in layers over a long period of time but is all of a piece, built all at one time out of clay adobes and faced with stone. Its cubic size has been calculated at 1,300,000 cubic yards, weighing some three million tons. Unfortunately the original silhouette was badly distorted by a dubious reconstruction carried out in 1903, when many of the facing stones were removed and the architect in charge rebuilt parts as he saw fit. The smaller Pyramid of the Moon was left untouched, however, and preserves its original proportions. Both pyramids originally were topped by temples on their summits. We have a good picture of the appearance of these temples from representations in murals and on pottery. They seem to have been relatively simple, rectangular buildings of post-and-lintel construction, similar to the temples shown in Mezcala miniatures, but with the distinctive attribute of having on their roofs enormous, crownlike ornamentations made of wood and straw, covered with a rich mosaic of flowers, and

fringed with brilliant quetzal feathers.

These feathers were favorite ornaments of the Classic and later periods; they are shown again and again in rich, cascading masses in the headdresses of gods and great personages. Since the quetzal, from whose tail they come, lives only in the highlands of southern Mexico and Guatemala, the widespread use of its feathers in early Classic times indicates that even then a very active trade was carried on through most of Middle America.

Trade also spread the cultural influence of Teotihuacán to the farthest reaches. There were very close relations and much stylistic interchange with the Gulf Coast region of Veracruz. At Cholula, where another huge pyramid of the same period as those of Teotihuacán exists, a whole temple-city fell under Teotihuacán influence. Monte Albán shows close stylistic ties, and the strongest Teotihuacán influence is also seen in the pottery of Kaminaljuyú, the great ancient center on the outskirts of Guatemala City. So far-reaching is the affinity expressed in pottery and figurine styles—as well as in architecture—that some archaeologists have speculated about Teotihuacán colonies as settlements of a commercial and religious character which imply not necessarily absolute political domination but perhaps intensive trade relations followed or paralleled by religious proselytizing. In any case, the enormous and unprecedented power of Teotihuacán as a religious, artistic and technical center created models that were followed widely all over Middle America (see page 143).

The great importance of Teotihuacán is that it is the first true city in ancient America. There has been much discussion about whether the Maya ceremonial centers were true cities or, rather, pilgrimage centers, and there is every evidence that Monte Albán was not a city but a giant acropolis of temples virtually without dwellings. Teotihuacán, however, was a true city, and even a metropolis. It possessed a ceremonial center of temples and courts for great rituals, and also a section for the habitations of the ruling elite, surrounded by the houses of the artisans and the rest of the population, and beyond these the home of the peasants. This basic type of town plan became traditional in Mexico. A thousand years later it was still followed when the newly civilized Aztecs built their capital of Tenochtitlán.

The spectacular accomplishments at Teotihuacán illustrate the grandiose vision and resolution of the priestly elite who could plan and complete monuments of such proportions. The tremendous mobilization of labor, the logistics of food supply, the unprecedented technical means that had to be devised were all without parallel. Yet Teotihuacán remained an open city, without walls or defenses. It was not far from the northern frontier that separated

Middle American civilization from the roving barbarian nomads, but it was the capital of an empire so powerful that it had no enemies capable of undertaking an attack. Military themes are absent in the art of Teotihuacán, and not until Toltec times are warriors depicted in the seats of power. Here only priests receive the unique glorification which art can bestow.

Teotihuacán's rulers probably were an elite of priests, drawn from a hereditary class. The priest-king was regarded as the living image of the deity, the impersonation of his presence among men, somewhat as the Tibetan Dalai Lama is believed to be the incarnation of Buddha. His powers must have been immense and imbued with the authority of divine sanction. With their knowledge of the calendar, the priesthood predicted the coming of the seasons and the rains, interpreted omens and augurs of good and evil, and propitiated the gods when necessary. The focus of their worship was the rain god Tlaloc, under whose special protection lay the vital corn crop.

A great body of skilled and increasingly specialized craftsmen and artists worked to supply the ritual needs for idols, offertorial urns, incense burners, sculpture and murals for temples and tombs, ceremonial garments and ornaments. The demand of the growing population for figurines soon grew so great that mass-production techniques were invented, especially the use of clay molds for the making of small idols for domestic worship and votive figurines for burials and offerings.

Most of the evidence of the spirit and religion of the great city comes from the splendid murals found here. These are true frescoes, painted on wet stucco in two-dimensional outlines filled in with bright, unshaded colors among which red, green, blue and yellow predominate. A sufficient number have been found to indicate that the art of painting flourished here on a grand scale. Among them are those of an important structure which is near the Pyramid of the Moon and is called the Temple of Agriculture, because of the subject of its murals, and others in buildings which are outside the main ceremonial center and are believed to have been residences of great personages.

Two main styles can be distinguished in the murals, with somewhat different themes. One is very formal and official and chiefly portrays the gods and the high priests in their service, surrounded by all their symbolic attributes, dressed in gorgeous paraphernalia and crowned by immense headdresses of long, cascading feathers. The rain god Tlaloc is represented with all his realm, the sea, waves, shells, starfish, and drops of rain falling from his hands onto the leaves and flowers that symbolized agriculture. Symbols that have not yet been identified may be glyphs detailing additional aspects of his glory and that of his priests. In one such mural is seen the first representation of the Feathered Serpent, the great god Quetzalcóatl, with whom high priests were identified until Aztec times. The highly stylized and iconographically rich representations of the gods in these hieratic murals are good evidence that a well-integrated, fully developed cosmic image and a coherent, clearly defined body of religious doctrine were already firmly established in early Classic times. Along with the rain god Tlaloc, the artists of Teotihuacán depicted heavenly cloud dragons and earth serpents, the mysterious "fat god" who disappeared again at the end of the Classic Period, the butterfly god, and various vegetation and corn deities. Almost all the members of the pantheon of later times were already represented here, with the happy exception of the bloodthirsty war gods, who were as yet undreamed of.

The other mural style of Teotihuacán was more realistic, more popular, and much less highly stylized. Although it too was completely religious in inspiration and theme, it recounted its pictorial tales in terms of the people and animals that inhabit this world. To this style belong the elegantly striding jaguars and coyotes at the entrance to the priestly residence found at Atetelco: elegant feathered felines and canines, out of whose mouths speech symbols appear in question-mark curls. These rise above stylized cloud forms from which life-giving rain is seen dropping onto the earth below. The subtlety and mystery of these splendid animals is enhanced by the restraint of the artists, who limited their use of color on them to four shades of red.

The most beautiful of this group of murals represents the rain

god's paradise, Tlalocán, the Blue House of Tlaloc, where the clouds gather and the souls of the dead meet. It is the most lyrical and realistic painting known in pre-Columbian art, and the most moving. On a mountain meadow encircled by water, scores of happy little human figurines are shown, painted in many gay colors. They are surrounded by a garden in which all kinds of delicious fruits and plants grow and where is found an abundance of birds, butterflies, fishes and all the good things nature can provide. Even the ground is strewn with shimmering green stones, precious jade lying around for the picking.

The inhabitants of paradise are shown engaged in every delightful pursuit. Some are bathing in the surrounding waters, others are shown diving into it, one is happily swimming on his back, and still another has just left the water and is wringing dry his long loincloth, from which drops of water are shown falling. On the edge of the water some rest under trees, while others pick flowers, and one man is eating an ear of corn. Off to one side, two seated people are playing a game with balls, while a third one looks on, perhaps as a referee. In the distance, implied by the upper reaches of the mural, four persons perform a strange kind of dance, a sort of conga line in which each participant reaches backward between his legs and clasps a hand of the man behind him. Most are shown with speech curls rising from their mouths, indicating conversation and song. Only one individual does not participate in all the happy activity. Heavy tears of overwhelming joy and emotion flow from his eyes, and from his lips rise five speech curls representing a long prayer of thanks to the rain god Tlaloc, as is indicated by the symbol of three shells above the speech curls. In his hand he holds a twig with fresh green leaves, showing that he is a man newly arrived in paradise. Ancient belief held that a dry twig placed in the hands of the deceased would blossom and grow fresh leaves when the bearer reached paradise.

The Teotihuacán frescoes set a style that was followed by all later Mexican murals and also by the codices, the great pictographic and hieroglyphic books of which so few survived the bookburning fury of the early Spanish missionaries. No codex of the Teotihuacán period has survived, but on stylistic evidence the leading Mexican archaeologist Alfonso Caso has concluded that by the time of the apogee of Teotihuacán, between A.D. 300 and 500, such books must have existed and served as models for the later Mixtec, Maya and Aztec codices that have come down to us.

The mural style was used also in decorating bowls of a characteristic form, cylindrical vessels resting on three rectangular feet and often covered with a lid. This form appears to have been developed in Teotihuacán, and to have spread from there as far as the Maya cities of Tikal and Kaminaljuyú in Guatemala. The most beautiful examples found at Teotihuacán are decorated with miniature frescoes, representing gods and priests with all their stylized attributes. To achieve this, a method called paint-cloisonné was used: the surface to be decorated was covered with a thin layer of fine clay, highly polished with the palm of the hand and allowed to set; the design then was cut out of the background and was scraped away, one color at a time, and the colors were applied to fill in the hollows; finally the completed surface was smoothed and polished off to the level of the original layer of fine clay. The colors used in these elaborate designs were chiefly soft tones of rose, turquoise green, ocher, gray and white. The technique appears to

have been used on wood and gourds as well as on clay vases, although only the latter have survived. Paint-cloisonné decorations that are found today are extremely fragile and can be preserved from crumbling into dust only by the skillful application of chemical binders to make the flaking colors adhere to the sides of the vessel.

All of the characteristics of Classic art found full expression at a very early date in Teotihuacán. The stark simplicity and restraint of Preclassic representations soon gave way to the Classic delight in luxurious ornamentation expressed in such details as the elaborate headdresses of massed fans of quetzal feathers. Art was now dedicated to the exaltation of priest-kings and to the unending representations of the gods of a growing pantheon. The dominant architectural style of alternating panels and slopes, which was to be constantly repeated in the construction of pyramids, was first developed at Teotihuacán. So were many other technical accomplishments that spread from here to other centers through trade and also as a result of the great dispersion of artists and craftsmen which occurred after the violent destruction of Teotihuacán at about A.D. 650.

The history of Teotihuacán is closely reflected in the development of its art, which falls into four distinct style periods known as Teotihuacán I, II, III and IV. They represent a long cultural continuity lasting almost a thousand years, from about 200 B.C. until well into the eighth century of the Christian Era, with formative, early classic, flourishing and decadent phases. The figurines of Teotihuacán I are still typical of the late Preclassic horizon in the Valley of Mexico: small, archaic clay figurines with slanted eyes, long noses and a unique, heavily emphasized prognathism. They are already shown wearing the typical Teotihuacán style of headdress with its extremely wide horizontal band, but generally they are quite crudely and sketchily made and have no special aesthetic merit. There is much evidence to indicate that the construction of the two great pyramids also belongs to this period.

Figurines now became very much more delicate and refined, with great attention being paid to the details of dress and ornamentation, capes, skirts, headbands, earplugs, necklaces and collars. Most were brilliantly painted in red, yellow and white, but unfortunately, fugitive colors were used, and only slight traces are still visible on the figurines that are found today. From this period, too, date the first of the life-size stone masks which are among the most beautiful and characteristic expressions of Teotihuacán art. These masks were fused in funeral ceremonies, tied to the great cloth bundles in which the dead were enveloped. The masks were cut off horizontally across the forehead so that the elaborate funeral headdress could rest on it, and the many drilled perforations on the sides served to attach the mask itself and to suspend from it earplug flares, necklaces, collars and other ornaments.

Covarrubias has pointed out that the use of stone masks comes

out of an Olmec tradition, traces of which are also visible in the typically Olmec V-shaped notch in the head of many clay figurines and in the use of small votive figurines of serpentine and jade. It is interesting to note that stone masks and figurines, considered such a typical cultural trait, have been found only in the Mexican highlands and were not present in other centers of Teotihuacán influence, such as Kaminaljuyú.

This was also the period of great stone sculpture, massive architectural monoliths that appear almost cubist in their schematic geometric stylization. The so-called Water Goddess is the outstanding example of the style: a huge thirteen-foot-high sculpture weighing some twenty-four tons. It demonstrates the powerful architectural sense of these ancient sculptors, who marvelously adapted the human form to geometric forms that follow the characteristic slope-and-panel pattern of Teotihuacán buildings. The fantastic stone heads that jut out from the bas-relief background on the Pyramid of Quetzalcóatl are carved in the same spirit although on a smaller scale. They represent symbolic combinations, alternately of jaguars and snakes, and of the stylized features of the rain god and the butterfly, which was considered one of his symbolic representatives. The famous white onyx offertorial vessel in the form of a plumed jaguar in the British Museum is another example of the style.

Toward the end of Teotihuacán II a new type of clay figurine was introduced, representing small, very slender personages in strange, dancing positions, which are referred to as "portrait type" figurines because their faces are so exquisitely modeled as to suggest individual portraits. They are dressed only in loincloths and wear no ornaments except for large earplugs. The heads, broken off the bodies, are found in abundance, but complete figurines are quite rare. Their varied stances and general appearance are very much like those of the happy residents of paradise shown in the mural of Tlalocán. There is every reason to think that such figurines, which are generally found in groups, were arranged to form realistic tableaux of the land of the dead, rather as a Christmas

crèche recalls the Nativity. Many of these figurines have hands carefully modeled so that they could hold the small twig that would come into leaf when they reached paradise.

During the Teotihuacán III period, the growing demand for clay figurines led to the use of clay molds to cast either heads or complete figurines. This led inevitably to a loss of aesthetic quality. This period also saw the invention of figurines with articulated arms and legs, giving them a truly doll-like aspect (see page 189).

Another invention of this period was the wheel—but it was used only on toys. Although the wheel was no secret to the ancient Indian cultures—wheeled toys have been found among the Maya, on the Gulf Coast as well as in the highland valleys of Mexico (see right)—no practical use was made of it by any pre-Columbian culture, possibly because, without draft animals, the wheel did not have much practical value. As for the great architectural monoliths, they could be moved more efficiently with the use of rollers.

Mural painting that began in the preceding period now reached a climax in the decoration of the numerous temples and palaces at Teotihuacán. The splendid cylindrical tripod bowls were manufactured and exported in great quantities, many of them with colorful fresco decorations and sculptured lids. At the same time, the decorative style became more elaborate, less architectural, and almost overloaded with sumptuous detail. A subtle transformation began to take place in the stone masks. They became more elegant, less square and more trapezoidal in shape, more refined but also somehow weaker, their features softer in character and expression. A new type of ceremonial brazier was made to represent the dead: huge, lidded vessels surmounted by enormous architectural structures made out of mold-made clay plaques delineating feathers, shields, birds, shells, butterflies, flowers and building elements. Together they form a kind of niche in which a clay mask representing the honored personage was displayed. Precious copal incense was burned, which ascended in smoke through the funnel-shaped lid of these grand braziers.

With the passage of centuries the small elite of priestly rulers

transformed itself into an increasingly large ruling class. Inspired guidance slowly gave way to oppression. Symptoms of decadence began to appear in their art, and their creative power was sapped and weakened. Internal discontent began, and the enormous prestige of the great priests slowly diminished. On the edges of its domain, however, primitive nomadic groups slowly absorbed elements of the culture that radiated from Teotihuacán. They formed permanent settlements, and there is evidence in mural paintings that warriors from such a group, the Otomí, may have served Teotihuacán as mercenaries in the defense of its frontiers against the northern barbarians. Then, suddenly, about A.D. 650, violent destruction overwhelmed Teotihuacán; it was sacked and burned, and the evidence is still there in the burned stucco and charred beams.

It is not known exactly who destroyed Teotihuacán. Most archaeologists tend to think that the city fell prey to one of the barbarian groups to the north who for so long had enviously eyed its riches, and who perhaps were helped by a revolt of the Otomí mercenaries. One theory suggests a revolt by an oppressed peasantry, increasingly put upon by a more and more demanding priesthood and perhaps pushed beyond endurance by crop failures and subsequent famines that occurred in spite of priestly sacrifices and predictions. Such events certainly seem to have contributed to the downfall of the glittering theocratic Maya cities two centuries later, but the best evidence of such popular revolutions—the smashed images of priests—is absent in Teotihuacán. The great metropolis, though probably weakened in advance by internal strains, definitely was destroyed by alien invaders.

After the abandonment of Teotihuacán, the great dispersal of its artists and craftsmen occurred. The culture of Teotihuacán continued at smaller centers on the western and southern shores of the great lake in the Valley of Mexico, especially at Azcapotzalco. Here a style known as Teotihuacán IV continued well into the ninth and even the tenth century, and in some places it actually seems to have overlapped the early part of the next great cultural period of the highlands, that of the Toltecs. Teotihuacán IV, as was perhaps to be expected, produced no innovations but continued the now frozen patterns of the preceding period. There was an increasingly sterile, unimaginative repetition of forms and ornaments. Headdresses overwhelm the little figurines, as if the outer trappings of a lost glory could replace its essence. Figures now were invariably made in molds, with little care being taken even to obtain neat castings. Gone were the elegant frescoed vases and the fine stone masks. Slowly the once great style fizzled out.

The noble heritage of Teotihuacán was not entirely lost, however. Its important discoveries lived on in the arts and crafts of such flourishing centers as Tajín in central Veracruz and Xochicalco in the Valley of Morelos. The gods of its pantheon continued to be worshiped, and the pattern of its murals was copied and recopied in codices for a thousand years to come. When powerful new invaders penetrated the Valley of Mexico three centuries later, the barbarian Toltecs built a great new culture by absorbing the still-living traditions of the old civilization and imbuing it with new life through their boundless energy.

THE ZAPOTECS

IN THE HIGHLAND VALLEYS OF OAXACA, a vigorous ancient people, the Zapotecs, created a highly individual culture which over a long period maintained close contacts with Teotihuacán as well as with the Olmecs and the Maya. The focus of their achievements was the most beautiful ceremonial site in ancient Mexico, Monte Albán ("White Mountain"). Situated on a man-made plateau on top of an isolated mountain at the junction of three valleys, it rises nearly a thousand feet above a green sea of fertility and is hemmed in by the steep mountain ranges that form the horizon.

Its origins date back to Preclassic times when an unknown genius, perhaps an Olmec priest, had the daring and vision to select this splendid place on which to build a city to his gods. Certainly the first beginnings show the strongest Olmec influence. The famous carved *Danzante* figures discussed earlier are purely Olmec in inspiration, as are the earliest offertorial urns found in Oaxaca. Typical are small clay braziers in the form of a human head, with characteristic Olmec traits such as the flaring, trapezoidal mouth reminiscent of a jaguar and a crying baby. Other vessels of this period—

which is known as Monte Albán I—are more closely related to those found at Tlatilco. Among these are zoomorphic bowls and long-necked vases representing birds, fish and jaguars, made of the gun-metal-gray clay which is a distinctive characteristic of Monte Albán pottery throughout the centuries.

The earliest temple found on Monte Albán is a relatively small structure made famous by the presence of the *Danzante* slabs. It was followed somewhat later by what appears to be an astronomical observatory, also decorated with stone slabs engraved with human figures of the *Danzante* type, but executed in a somewhat later style. They are accompanied by interesting early glyphs some of which represent the names of vanquished tribes or cities. These comparatively modest beginnings were followed by a series of buildings planned with vision and foresight and executed over a period of centuries. There are small and large temple bases, ascended by sweeping ceremonial stairways and faced by grand ceremonial courts. One many-chambered building may have been a priestly palace, and there is a magnificent ball court for the ritual game which the Zapotecs shared with the other cultures of the

Classic Period. All of these splendid structures are grouped around a majestic central plaza which was carved out of the mountaintop and measures just short of a mile in length and some 850 feet in width. It is a truly grandiose architectural conception. Today its carefully excavated ruins make the Acropolis of Athens look modest and the Roman Forum somewhat haphazard.

Unlike Teotihuacán, Monte Albán was not a true city, but a temple-city of the gods and of the dead. The great crowds which filled the courts and plazas and attended the spectacular rituals on the great ceremonial occasions were drawn from the surrounding countryside and probably included pilgrims from far away. The tradition of long-distance pilgrimages is an old one in the world of the Indians and dates back to very ancient times. At the shrine of the Black Christ of Esquipulas in Guatemala—which probably replaces a much older pagan shrine—pilgrims have been reported by modern anthropologists from as far away as central Mexico, Ecuador and Peru. These were Indian pilgrims without the means to pay for modern transportation and who must have walked, worked and begged their way over enormous and even today often roadless and "impassable" distances. There is every reason to think that this represents the continuation of a very old custom dating from long before the Conquest.

A unique aspect of Monte Albán was its function as a necropolis, a city of the dead. Important chambered tombs have been found hidden inside Maya temple pyramids, and deep shaft and chamber tombs are known in the late archaic cultures of western Mexico. But Monte Albán is the only true necropolis found in Mexico. One tomb chamber was placed next to the other until even the number of excavated graves (a small proportion of the total known to exist) runs close to two hundred. The entire sides of the mountain of Monte Albán are studded with such tombs, hewn out of the living rock like so many caves—the caves from which, according to the legends, their ancestors had come, and into which their dead were laid to rest to join them. The best efforts of Zapotec artists went into the construction and furnishing of these tombs. It is from them

that we have obtained most of our knowledge of their culture, as well as their finest objects.

During the height of the Classic Period the entire walls of tombs were often covered with murals stylistically related to the formal frescoes of Teotihuacán, but using somewhat simpler and more vigorous forms. Elaborate glyph inscriptions record still-undeciphered dates and details. Most characteristic, however, are the elaborate clay urns found in all tombs. They represent the high point of Zapotec art, and in their development we can best follow the evolution of the style of Monte Albán.

The Preclassic period of Monte Albán I saw the first appearance of vases representing the rain god known to the Zapotecs as Cosijo, whose face is composed of human, jaguar and serpent elements and has a characteristic forked tongue, representing lightning. The forms of these vessels were still very simple, straight-sided and decorated with fine incised lines. The gray color typical of Oaxaca pottery was a very light gray at this period, while in later periods it often darkened to a battleship gray. Also part of this horizon

are small votive female figurines, the local counterpart of the type found in all of the early archaic cultures.

Monte Albán II is the period of the end of the Preclassic horizon. The strange arrow-shaped building in the middle of the central plaza on Monte Albán, which probably was an astronomical observatory and is decorated with some sixty stone slabs of the later *Danzante* type, was built at this time. The small clay urns of the first period continued to be made but on a larger and more elaborate scale, until the human form dominated the urn form and they became transformed into true sculpture. They represent distinguished, aristocratic-looking personages with great slanting eyes, half-open, almost speaking mouths, and long-fingered hands held in dramatic ritual gestures. Other urns represent the rain god and the important corn god called Pitao Cozobi, recognized by his attributes of corncobs and tassels. To this period also belongs a superlative jade mask of the bat god made of various pieces of dark-green jade carefully fitted together into a powerful, haunting image.

The simplicity of forms and the sculptural power of Monte Albán II are the apogee of Zapotec art, at least to the eyes of our time. The increasing elaboration which occurred during the Monte Albán III period is technically admirable, and resulted in huge, dramatic urns, but in all their rich detail they never quite equaled the dramatic vigor of Monte Albán II. The taste of our parents and grandparents, however, preferred the flowery style of the later periods, and most of the examples one sees in museums and in older publications are of later times. It is also interesting to note that the later Monte Albán urns were appreciated and collected at a time when the art of other pre-Columbian cultures was still little understood and less admired.

Monte Albán III was contemporary with the flowering of Teotihuacán and Classic Maya art, and it shares many traits with them. The great urns of this period generally portrayed personages seated cross-legged, with their hands on their knees, their faces raised upward in contemplation. They are shown wearing enormous, intricate headdresses with stylized masks of gods and totemic animals, great earplugs, bracelets, necklaces, collars and capes which fall regally across their sholders. Other urns personify gods and the great totemic animals, the jaguar and the bat. Among the Zapotecs, the bat was associated with the corn god, whose form and motifs occur again and again in their art.

The urns of the first part of this period, known as Monte Albán III-A, were still sharply carved after drying and just before firing, producing vigorous, clear-cut planes. During the latter part of the period, called Monte Albán III-B, clay molds came into use, and their increasing application worked to the detriment of sculptural quality and originality. The forms became set and were endlessly and unimaginatively repeated, while the emphasis on the great urns shifted from their human features and their sculptural integrity to an overconcentration on iconographic and decorative details of ornament.

The decline of the Classic Period saw the abandonment of Monte Albán as a ceremonial center, although it continued to be used as a place of burial. The weakened, decadent style of this time, known as Monte Albán IV, repeats the features of Monte Albán III-B and introduces only one new form, small votive vessels in the form of the paw of a jaguar with its claws extended.

By the end of this period—generally placed between A.D. 1200 and 1400—the old forms had become lifeless. The Zapotecs eventually adopted the style developed to the north of them by a culture known as Mixtec or Mixteca-Puebla, and to this culture the Zapotecs contributed some of its finest achievements, at Mitla and in the treasures of the famous Tomb 7 at Monte Albán. But this belongs to the Historic Period, and will be discussed in a later chapter.

The eminently dignified art of the Classic Zapotecs reflects their always sober, serious spirit. There was little playfulness here, but great aristocratic dignity and architectural balance. It is a perfect embodiment of the priestly thinking and vision that created the breathtaking temple-city of Monte Albán.

VERACRUZ: REMOJADAS

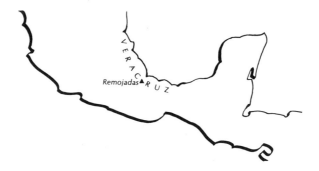

FOR MANY YEARS ONLY A FEW RARE fragments of "Smiling Heads" were known of the extraordinary clay art that flourished in central Veracruz during the Classic Period. There was much speculation as to what the heads might have been—one archaeologist suggested that they must have been architectural ornaments—and they were usually called Totonac, after the people who inhabited this region at the time of the Spanish Conquest. During the last few years, however, an extraordinary amount of excavation has been done in this region, and it has uncovered quantities of figurines, as well as superb large-scale clay sculpture, which have revealed an exciting, complex and aesthetically sophisticated culture. This culture is now often called Remojadas, after one of the chief sites of the famous recent finds.

The beginnings of the culture go back to archaic, Preclassic times and are typified by small, solid figurines made of the sand-colored clay of this region. Some of the earliest figurines are already decorated with face and body markings painted with the shiny black tar which occurs naturally in this region and whose use is a unique local specialty. A remarkable feature of this material is that it seems to be virtually impervious to aging. When cleaned of the accumulated mud and dirt of the ages, its jet-black surface shines as brilliantly as the day it was applied.

Typical of the Preclassic horizon in this region are a variety of human and animal effigy vessels with a beautifully burnished surface, often with some black tar used to define the eyes, mouth and other details. An interesting feature of these vessels is their technical and stylistic similarity to certain Peruvian vessels, whose spouts and handles form one unit, a type also found at Tlatilco and early Monte Albán tombs. The Remojadas effigy vessels generally represent seated men and women, and monkeys, badgers, birds, armadillos, and domestic animals.

During the transitional stage between the Preclassic and Classic Periods, the production of archaic-style solid clay figurines continued, but on a larger, more impressive scale. A typical early form is the cross-legged figurine, hands resting on knees. The work is marvelously simplified, stylized—a slab body, two diagonal beams for arms, and an intertwined pretzel shape to indicate the crossed legs. Slowly, however, individual character began to replace impersonal stylization; the stiff body forms were relaxed, and more attention was paid to anatomic realism in the limbs and torso, and the figures were graced with splendidly expressive heads, which foreshadowed the life-size, portrait heads of the Classic flowering.

The Classic Period itself was heralded by the appearance of the early type of Smiling Head figurine. These are generally about ten inches tall and represent rather stiffly postured young boys dressed in loincloths and chest bands, standing with their legs apart and arms spread wide. Their stylized faces have a grinning expression —not yet a true smile—and flat, trapezoid headdresses emphasize their flattened heads, which reflect the real-life custom of head-binding, a widespread practice in the Classic Period, especially on the Gulf Coast and among the Maya; like so many other customs of that period, it seems to have originated among the Olmecs.

The early Smiling Head figurines usually contain a whistle,

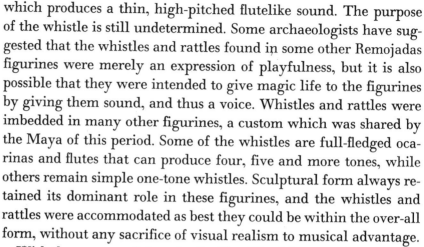

which produces a thin, high-pitched flutelike sound. The purpose of the whistle is still undetermined. Some archaeologists have suggested that the whistles and rattles found in some other Remojadas figurines were merely an expression of playfulness, but it is also possible that they were intended to give magic life to the figurines by giving them sound, and thus a voice. Whistles and rattles were imbedded in many other figurines, a custom which was shared by the Maya of this period. Some of the whistles are full-fledged ocarinas and flutes that can produce four, five and more tones, while others remain simple one-tone whistles. Sculptural form always retained its dominant role in these figurines, and the whistles and rattles were accommodated as best they could be within the over-all form, without any sacrifice of visual realism to musical advantage.

With the passage of time the Smiling Head figurines became less stylized, more realistic and considerably larger, up to twenty inches in height. In contrast to what happened in other Classic cultures as a consequence of the increased use of molds in the manufacture of figurines, aesthetic quality improved immeasurably with the use of extremely refined molds by the artists of the Remojadas culture. They achieved the first true smile portrayed by any ancient culture, a radiantly happy and touchingly human expression, which they were able to portray in its full range from a cryptic, philosophical smile to impish, infectious laughter.

These enchanting figurines now represented both boys and girls, sometimes nude except for the ever present, elaborately detailed headdress, sometimes dressed in chest band and loincloth, sometimes in skirts or full-length dresses of rich textiles delicately reproduced with their complicated weaves and patterns. Their legs often show the bent-knee stance reminiscent of Olmec figurines and their hands hold musical rattles or cover their faces as if in embarrassment or awe. Sometimes the headdress is only a ribbon-like band laid in an elegant question-mark curl across a plain wide cap, but more commonly it is covered with symbolic designs featuring monkeys, pelicans or elaborate scroll-design patterns representing stylized serpents. The figurines usually were made out of two molds, one for the face and another for the remainder of the front of the figure, while the back of the head and the body were always filled out by hand. They are hollow and, unlike their earlier prototypes, they are seldom equipped with whistles. Originally they were usually painted with red, yellow, blue and white paint, of which unfortunately only traces remain today.

There is as yet no conclusive evidence as to what the Smiling Head figurines represent or why they were made. Some clues are provided by the fact that while complete figurines are quite rare their broken-off heads have been found in much larger quantities. This leads to the conclusion that they may have been produced

in enormous quantities to be offered to the gods as sacrifices in rituals which called for the destruction of the body and the interment of the head alone. The fact that the comparatively few human sacrifices offered during the Classic Period often were of children and the belief that sacrificial victims were immediately granted eternal, superlatively blissful existence among the gods might explain why the Smiling Head faces show such ecstatic happiness and why virtually all represent children. If indeed they served as substitutes for human sacrifice, like Abraham's ram, their happy smile is doubly understandable and all the more evidence of the high level of civilization attained by the people of Remojadas.

Other typical Remojadas figurines are little ones of elaborately dressed women seated on high benches or standing in wooden gates shaped like hockey goals. One amusing example shows two such personages seated face to face on a bench, with a bowl or brazier resting between them. The women always wear knee-length skirts and short capes, topped off by wide-banded headdresses, each with five or six huge, stylized feathers rising from the back and a bird decorating the front. They wear large earplugs, necklaces and elaborate sandals, and their teeth often appear to have been filed. The lower half of the face from the tip of the nose to the chin is generally covered with a half mask. The Mexican archaeologist Alfonso Medellin Zenil has suggested that these figurines represent the goddess Tlazolteotl, the Earth Mother, wearing some of the attributes of Xipe Totec, the flayed god of vegetation. The latter deity, judging by his frequent representation in the art of Remojadas, enjoyed special devotion in this region, notwithstanding the gruesome rites involved in his worship. These called for the priest who represented the deity to wear a new skin, lifted from a sacrificial victim, symbolizing the new skin of young plants. Happily the representations of Xipe in this culture are highly stylized; it is not until Aztec times that statues show in all their full, horrifying impact all the details of these ancient rites of spring.

Another type of Remojadas figure is characterized by a peculiar

style of hairdress, with a part in the middle, and the sides sweeping down like a Napoleonic hat. These figurines are generally shown with round, decorative patches on both cheeks and are seated in the cross-legged, Buddha-like position so often favored by Remojadas sculptors. Other subjects include a wide variety of animals, including very expressionistic figurines of dogs and coyotes, their features marked with black tar. Some of these took the form of wheeled toys.

The extraordinarily wide range of Remojadas clay sculpture includes many dramatic representations of the deities and mythical figures which crowded the imaginative pantheon of this priestly age. There are huge anthropomorphic braziers almost entirely covered with jet-black tar. In other figures this shiny substance was used more sparingly, to give life to the faces and eyes. There are the legendary women warriors, the Cihuateteo, nude above the waist, wearing long skirts with wide belts, huge earplugs and sumptuous, towering headdresses. Dignified, aristocratic priests were shown in the full garments of their office, representing the personification of their gods. Often they stand with arms spread out in giving and consoling gestures, their hands beautifully detailed and fingers held in ritual positions whose exact meanings still remain to be interpreted. Details of headdresses, garments and ornaments were represented with loving attention to all the intricate symbolic details, but the figures were so well conceived as complete sculptural entities that the human features are never lost or crushed by an overload of ritualistic paraphernalia, as was sometimes the case in the art of other cultures during the height of the Classic Period.

The sculptors of Remojadas reached their apogee in life-size clay figures, which are the most splendid accomplishments in this medium in ancient America. As technical feats alone, they are tremendous achievements considering the small, low-temperature ovens then available and the structural problems that had to be overcome in supporting these heavy figures internally. But their creators' aesthetic triumphs far outdistance their technical victories. These artists not only overcame the restrictions of their material, they also went beyond the limitations of their time and place to create masterpieces that speak in universal human terms. One aristocratic head is the portrait of a man, whose sensitivity and intelligence still radiate. It is the work of an artist whose power and immediacy still touch us today.

A tragedy for the art of Remojadas was the custom of ceremonially breaking a figure before it was interred. This was based on an ancient Indian belief going back to earliest archaic times that a vessel or a figure had to be ritually "killed" by being broken or having a hole punched in it so that its spirit would be freed to accompany the dead on their voyage to the after life. This rite has caused some of the most tragic breaks in magnificent Maya vases and Olmec jades, but in Veracruz the destructive effects of this ritual were aggravated by the fact that the figures were buried directly in the heavy soil instead of being placed in roofed chambers as at Monte Albán or in Jalisco and Colima. Thus, during burial and again during excavation, Veracruz figures twice ran the risk of serious breakage, with the result that there are virtually no unbroken figures larger than about twelve inches. Unscrupulous restorers have taken to "cannibalizing" figures and making impressive counterfeits out of ill-assorted fragments found in careless excavations. To hide their traces, they often smear a thick wash of finely ground clay fragments in solution over an entire figure,

inside and out, so that only X rays can show the repairs that have been made.

Another very beautiful figurine style has been found at a site, not far from Remojadas, called El Faisan, by which name the style is now known. They were made of a fine cream-colored clay lavishly painted with distinctive shades of red and black, then heavily burnished to a high gloss. The figurines are hollow, but were never decorated on the always perfunctorily completed back; only the front and the shallow sides were painted and burnished. Many have whistles imbedded in their backs; and some have pebbles enclosed in their hollow interiors, so that they can be used as rattles. Virtually all of the figurines of this style represent women, and the most charming of them are shown riding on a swing.

The best available evidence indicates that the earliest horizon at Remojadas dates back before 500 B.C., and that the first small Smiling Head figurines made their appearance around 100 B.C. The culture reached its climax during the early part of the Classic Period and underwent a distinct decline after A.D. 600. The quality of the Smiling Head figures rapidly became poorer. The crude, coarsely made figurines which were made then totally lack the enchantment of their predecessors. At about the time of the fall of Teotihuacán, the creative center seems to have shifted to the north, to the region of the great temple city of Tajín in northern Veracruz.

VERACRUZ:
YOKES, HACHAS AND PALMAS

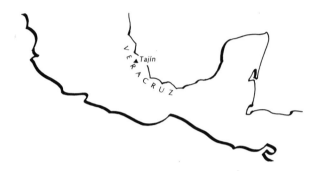

THE CLASSIC CULTURE THAT FLOURISHED in the lush tropical plains of the Gulf Coast is typified by the three unique forms of stone sculpture. All three were made to be worn by priests and dignitaries during rituals and ceremonies, but their function remained obscure until recently. These remarkable objects are still widely known by the misnomers given them at the turn of the century, when they first began to be collected by the then governor of the State of Veracruz, Dehesa. Because their symbolism and use were misunderstood, they were originally called yokes (as in the yokes placed about the necks of oxen); *hachas* (Spanish for axes); and *palmas* (for palm-shaped stones). Their actual function was analyzed and documented only some fifteen years ago by the noted American archaeologist Gordon F. Ekholm, who proved, in the face of considerable initial skepticism and ridicule, that yokes had been worn as belts by participants in the ritual ball game, and that *palmas* and the stone heads referred to as *hachas* had also been made to be worn at the waist, resting on heavy yokelike belts, during ceremonies and sacrifices by priests and other participants.

Little other sculpture was produced by the stone carvers of this period. These three forms became the focus of all their efforts and the embodiment of their finest achievements. The oldest of the three forms appears to have been the yoke. Perfectly plain, unsculptured stone yokes have been found in burials together with late Preclassic pottery, and other yokes still show strong Olmec influences in their style of carving. They continued to be made until the very end of the Classic Period, generally carved out of very hard, fine stones almost always green in color, and often polished to a high, jewellike sheen. They are all of about the same size, just right for wearing, some eighteen inches long and twelve inches wide, with an opening between six and eight inches wide; one variation, known as a closed yoke, has a stirruplike, flat closing bar between the two ends. Their design and execution represent some of the finest attainments of Indian art. Their intricate conceptions include crouching frogs and jaguars, the head at the center of the curve, the feet at the ends. Human figures and deities are shown adapted to the same stylized position on some yokes, and still others represent double-headed serpents and infinitely intricate variations of these themes. Many yokes also depict human profiles carved in low relief on the two flat ends. Others reproduce woven designs clearly showing that they follow original prototypes of basketry or leather.

Yokes were worn sideways around the waist so that the center rested on one hip and the two ends met at the other. This way they are actually not very uncomfortable to carry. Some years ago the author saw an Indian digger bring in a yoke from the field by wearing it in the ancient fashion around his waist. When asked why he had chosen this method the man explained that this had proved to be the easiest and most comfortable way of carrying the stone sculpture.

The original wearers of the yokes were the players of the ancient ceremonial ball game; they are often shown with such heavy belts in murals, bas-reliefs and clay figurines. The sacred game was played all over Middle America, but it appears to have originated

on the Gulf Coast, where the rubber used in the solid round ball
was first known and produced. The game and its intricate rules
were carefully described by the sixteenth-century Spanish missionary Fray Diego Durán, who observed it still being played by
the Aztecs. A rubber ball as big as a bowling ball was kept in the
air as long as possible by two contending teams, who were allowed
to return the ball only with their hips, buttocks and knees. Each
team tried to force the ball into the dead end of the I-beam-shaped
court, on the opposing team's side, so that it could not be returned.
A later refinement was the installation of doughnut-shaped rings
in a vertical position on the walls of the sunken ball courts, the
objective being to propel the ball through these. Other additionals
include the still mysterious, beautifully stylized "padlock stones,"
whose handles indicate that they may have been passed from
player to player during the game, or may have been used as markers during its progress. The game itself seems to have been both
a sport and a ritual performance with cosmic significance.

The second major form of wearable stone ornament is the type
originally known as *hachas*—stone heads, human and animal—
also worn at the waist. Their construction clearly shows that some
were worn in heavy yokelike belts that had notched openings to
hold the heads, while others have a protruding tenon at the back
so that they could be fitted into a specially slotted carrying belt.
These heads all date from the Classic Period, but they represent
a type of ornament that was already shown in bas-relief on very
early stelae. It has been suggested that they were stylized deriva-
tions of the trophy heads similarly displayed during earlier head-
hunting times.

The ornamental stone heads range from five to fifteen inches in
height. Some are completely flat, slablike stones with bas-relief
carving, while others are thicker and almost three-dimensional in
execution. They were generally carved out of fine-grained stone
and were painted red with cinnabar or cochineal before burial.
The rich fantasy and intricate symbolism of Classic iconography
is beautifully demonstrated by the endless variety of heads, in-

cluding those of parrots, pelicans, dolphins, monkeys and human skulls. Some are simple and realistic, others elaborately combine the features of different mythical personages. Some of the most interesting of the stone heads show the living face of a man or an animal on one side, and a skull on the other, a characteristic expression of the profound Indian involvement with the duality of nature, the lurking presence of death in the midst of life.

Ornamental stone heads have an even wider distribution than yokes. They have been found in the highland valleys of Mexico, in the Maya lowlands at Palenque, and especially on the Pacific slope of Guatemala and El Salvador. The Mexican archaeologist Jiménez Moreno has explained the extraordinarily widespread, but always comparatively isolated, occurrence of these stone heads as a result of the great migrations that occurred during the tremendous upheavals at the end of the long, peaceful theocratic Classic Period. A great civilized people known as the Pipil ("princes," or "nobles"), who lived in Veracruz—and also dominated the highland center of Cholula in the Valley of Puebla—were forced out by the "Historic Olmecs" from Tabasco. This produced a great migration of the Pipil, who spoke a variation of the great Nahuatl language, later also spoken by the Aztecs, toward the south and southeast. Their migration route went along the Gulf Coast, through the Maya city of Palenque (which, it is believed by some, they destroyed), across the Isthmus of Tehuantepec and then down along the Pacific Coast of Guatemala and Honduras as far as Nicaragua and the Nicoya peninsula of Costa Rica. This route of the Pipil coincides exactly both with the distribution of yokes and ornamental stone heads and with small islands of populations who still speak the early Nahuatl dialect and who may have been left in the wake of the great Pipil migration.

An important and apparently local later variation of the basic type of ornament represented by the stone heads are the *palmas*. These have been found only in central Veracruz, where they seem to have replaced the stone heads during the late Classic Period. Although other forms were abandoned, *palmas* were made here

well into the early Historic Period, when Toltec motifs began to make their appearance in some of them.

Unlike the stone heads, *palmas* were not fitted into special carrying belts but were worn with their fitted concave base resting on the wide, rounded tops of yokes or similar belts. Bas-reliefs in the temple-city of Tajín show them clearly in use during ceremonies, leaning slightly forward from the chest. Their size varies from an almost miniature six inches to truly regal examples of more than twenty-four inches in height. Their subject matter ranges from pure, abstract forms to stylized bundles of feathers and richly detailed representations of heads and figures, of humans and of animals such as pelicans, eagles, deer, monkeys and alligators. One interesting example shows a priest in full regalia wearing just such a *palma*. Here again it has been suggested that the stone *palmas* we know, like the ornamental stone heads and the yokes, may have had wooden counterparts that were more commonly worn but which have not survived the destructive action of the earth in a tropical rain-forest climate.

These three great forms represent the high point of the stone sculpture of the Classic Period. Their great dignity and magnificent symbolism are perfect reflections of the spirit of this priestly age. Their ingenious adaptation of every kind of human and animal form to the exigencies of ritually prescribed functional forms are triumphs of imagination by the great artists of the period.

An important basic design that appears on all three types of stone objects is the rounded square scroll, which in continuous flowing convolutions forms sometimes the background, sometimes the dominant motif in their elaborate decorations. This style, which has been defined as the Classic Scroll Style, has very early roots. It seems to come out of an elaboration of Olmec forms and symbolism—out of jaguar masks, sky dragons and cloud motifs. Early forms of this appear in such Olmec art as the famous rock carvings at Chilcancingo in Morelos. The Scroll Style was well adapted to the taste of a growing priestly elite eager to have religious subject matter represented in a manner so stylized and disguised that it could be understood only by the initiated. Thus it soon turned into virtually abstract decoration in which the subject can be recognized only with difficulty.

One of the most beautiful expressions of the Scroll Style is found in the glorious onyx and marble bases made by the Maya of the Ulúa Valley in Honduras during the late Classic Period, around A.D. 1000. These cylindrical vessels are covered with elegantly

flowing scrolls which at the same time depict and disguise the mask of a deity. Realistic, high-relief animal sculptures on the sides serve as handles. These vessels also point up the surprising similarity, in concept and execution, between the Scroll Style and the art of pre-Buddhist China, especially the jades and bronzes of the Shang and Chou dynasty.

Whether there was indeed any connection in civilized times between the Far East and America is a difficult, tantalizing question. No absolute proofs exist, but there are so many straws in the wind —in the form of quite extraordinary and otherwise inexplicable similarities of odd cultural details—that it seems safe to conclude that some contacts must have taken place, although of probably limited cultural impact. The question has been studied in detail and at length by Gordon F. Ekholm, Robert von Heine-Geldern, and Miguel Covarrubias. Their reports make some of the most fascinating reading ever presented in the dry and cautious language of archaeologists.

Among the clues to which they have pointed are such general similarities as the exceptional value attached to jade on both sides of the Pacific. The Indian game of *patolli* is virtually an exact counterpart of the southern Asian game of pachisi and has the same cosmic implications. Teotihuacán tripod pottery bowls follow a form which appears to be an exact copy of Chinese bronze vessels. The lotus motif is common among the Maya as a design element on borders; it is also found in India and Indochina. What is most unusual, however, is that both in America and in Asia the rhizome—the rootlike stem that grows underground—is made into a basic element of the motif. Furthermore, it is stylized on the two continents in the same unrealistic manner, as an undulating creeper. Still other similarities are the use of huge parasols as insignia of royalty and rank; the architectural device of ceremonial stairways flanked by serpent balustrades; the *volador* game, in which a man at the end of a long rope attached to the top of a tall pole seems to fly around the pole; and similar conceptions of hell and the punishments there inflicted.

THE MAYA

THE SUMMIT OF THE CLASSIC AGE—and, indeed, of all cultural achievement in ancient America—was reached by the Maya in their great temple-cities. These are spread like a chain of jewels from Palenque in the west, up into the Yucatán peninsula and down through British Honduras and Guatemala to Copán. They were first rediscovered for modern man in 1839 by the American explorer John Lloyd Stephens and the English artist Frederick Catherwood, whose excellent, detailed drawings revealed the splendors of the Maya ruins in the midst of the dense jungle. The publication of these drawings sparked an interest in this magnificent culture, and that interest has continued without interruption to this day. The Maya were the first of the ancient cultures to be thoroughly studied. Intensive explorations were carried out as early as the Eighties and Nineties of the last century by the Englishman Alfred P. Maudslay, and later by the Germans Teobert Maler and Eduard Georg Seler and the American Alfred Marston Tozzer. Since then there has been an uninterrupted procession of scientists.

The most astounding aspect of the Maya is that they built their greatest cities in a dense tropical rain forest, where every foot of ground had to be laboriously cleared with stone tools, where an always-encroaching jungle had to be constantly pushed back, and where the soil is so poor and thin that after a very few crops it had to be surrendered again to the jungle and a new clearing had to be laboriously hacked out. To have had enough energy left after all that to build their dazzling temple-cities remains an unparalleled achievement.

The Maya were a people of a distinct physical type, with high cheekbones and fleshy, hooked noses, whose aquiline form was emphasized at times by the wearing of artificial nosepieces to carry the bridge of the nose above the eyebrows to the forehead. With their heavy-lidded eyes, their drooping lower lips, their artificially deformed and lengthened foreheads, they epitomized the aristocratic beauty depicted in the art of the Classic Period.

Their priests and chiefs wore their hair in elegant and complex styles, cut into long locks that were twisted and built into elaborate hairdresses adorned with flowers, tubes of jade, and the brilliant feathers of the quetzal. In their ears they wore jade earplug flares with central ornaments of long jade tubes ending in small jade blossoms. They wore jade rings on their fingers, and their wrists and ankles were covered with cuffs and leggings of row upon row of emerald-green jade beads. Wide collars of beads, often with votive masks suspended, were worn on the chest. Their garments were short skirts, decorative loincloths, and elaborate ceremonial capes of complicated textiles or feather mosaics. They must have made a dazzling spectacle as they walked across the ceremonial courts and up the steep stairways of temple pyramids, in slow and pompous processions, accompanied by the sound of song and music and the smell of burning copal incense.

Much of Maya art was dedicated to the apotheosis of their great priests, to their gods and to their fabulous concept of time. In glorifying their leaders, the Maya artists became involved with concepts of naturalistic representation which had never occurred to the artists of other Indian cultures. They tackled successfully such daring subjects as the realistic foreshortening of figures, and group compositions with persons in naturalistic poses. The ever-present gods in Maya monuments are personified by the fierce sky serpents and dragons that hover above, and the fantastic earth monsters that crouch below the solemn priestly figures on the stelae.

Much of the realism and the exciting sculptural quality of Mayan art is obscured at first by the heavy crowding of glyphs, which to the unaccustomed eye seem to overwhelm so many Maya monuments. These glyphs are evidence of the Maya's unique obsession with time. Their best minds were preoccupied with the concept of the never-ending flow of days from the eternity of the past into the eternity of the future. But especially the past. From the past they strove to learn the constellations of deities who had dominated each time segment for good or evil, and from the return of these constellations they predicted the future inclination of the deities toward man.

Each cycle of time—day and night, week and month, and all the other segments into which the Maya divided time—was the special burden of one special god, who carried it across the sky as his appointed load. Many of the time glyphs clearly show a god carrying on his back the great burden of his time cycle, steadied by a tumpline across his forehead, just as Indians today carry heavy loads.

In pursuit of the mystery of time, Maya priests for centuries observed the occurrence of eclipses, equinoxes, solstices, and the courses of the sun, the moon and especially the planet Venus. They worked out an intricate calendar based on ever-repeating cycles ranging from a single day, called *kin*, to the *uinal* (a month of 20 days), *tun* (one year of 18 *uinals*, or 360 days), *katun* (7,200 days, or 20 years) and *baktuns* (a cycle of 20 *katuns*, or 400 years of 360 days, approximately 394 years of our reckoning). The basic ritual period that guided religious observances was a cycle of 260 days. With their understanding of the divisions of time and the

deities which governed those divisions, the priests could ascertain the favorable and the unpromising times for the undertaking of every kind of activity.

The Maya's interest in time produced a calendar far more accurate than the European calendar in use at the time of the Conquest, and led them to extraordinary achievements in mathematics. They evolved a duodecimal system and discovered the use of the zero long before the Hindus and Arabs did. The reckoning of time held no terror for them. Calculations of cycles up to 8,000 years are commonly recorded. On one monument in the Maya city of Quiriguá, accurate computations sweep back ninety million years; on another, four hundred million years. These are correct computations stating correctly the day and month positions, comparable for example to calculations in our calendar giving the dates on which Easter would have fallen at equivalent distances in the past. They were made a thousand years before Bishop Ussher in

seventeenth-century England placed the creation of the world at
4004 B.C.!

Throughout the great Classic Period the Maya calendar continued to be checked in observatories, which are found in almost
all the Maya cities. A great stone monument in Copán commemo-
rates an astronomical congress held in A.D. 773 by sixteen priestly
representatives of Maya cities. In fact, it has been suggested that
the Maya were stopped from developing their glyphic writing into
a true phonetic script by just this need to have a system of calendric and astrological notation which could be used by priests of
various linguistic groups.

The problem of correlating Maya calendric inscriptions with
our own calendar is still not fully solved. A number of detailed
correlations have been worked out, one by the American archaeologist Herbert Spinden and another by a succession of archaeolo-

gists and known as the Goodman-Martinez-Thompson correlation. There is a difference of about 260 years between the respective readings of these two major correlations, and opinion has varied as to which is the more accurate. At one point the Spinden correlation was widely discredited. Then came the first Carbon-14 tests, which seemed to re-establish its accuracy. Now new evidence suggests that the Goodman-Martinez-Thompson correlation is the more accurate. In this book the Goodman-Martinez-Thompson dates have been used.

To mark the passage of important dynastic events and intervals of time, towering stone stelae were erected by the Maya. These monoliths, some of them standing thirty feet high, became the most important and representative expression of Maya sculpture. Carved with amazing skill and absolute mastery of immense stone surfaces, they express the refined taste of the Classic Maya for

intricate, florid pictorial detail combined with majestic glyph recitals of great events. The basic technique used is that of bas-relief applied to the various sides of a solitary stela. But in the greatest of them—such as the massive eighth-century stelae of Copán in Honduras—the entire monolith is treated as a single sculptural entity, and the dominant human figure emerges in fully rounded high relief.

The Maya also were superb wood carvers, although only very few pieces have survived in the jungle climate. The most impressive are the magnificent zapote wood lintels from Tikal, carved in bas-relief and originally painted in vivid colors.

Some of the most beautiful and moving Maya sculpture that has survived was modeled in lime stucco. This material seems to have been used only by the Maya, who employed it chiefly for building decorations and reliefs. Two magnificent stucco heads were found among the offerings in an impressive tomb discovered at Palenque in 1954 (see frontispiece). The sensitivity and restrained dignity of these two young faces still touch us today. They are the consummation of the centuries of aristocratic refinement and cultural progress which produced both the noble subjects and the accomplished artists who have captured the very breath of life.

The tomb in which they were found was the most elaborate yet uncovered in America. In the magnificence of its contents, as well as in the excitement produced by its discovery, it ranks with the tomb of Tutankhamen. It was found by the Mexican archaeologist Alberto Ruz, who had noticed that a large slab in the floor of the inner room of a building called the Temple of the Inscriptions had what seemed to be finger holes in it, suggesting that it could be raised. It proved to be the trap door that led to a narrow vaulted stairway descending into the heart of the pyramid. It had been purposely filled with rubble and earth on completion of the burial. It took three years of careful excavating to remove the solidly packed blockading material. After various turns, the stairway led down about sixty feet, to a large vaulted room whose walls were decorated by nine stucco reliefs representing the gods of the under-

world. The middle of the floor was occupied by a huge stone sarcophagus the lid of which weighed some five tons and was decorated with a superb bas-relief showing a great personage reclining
on an earth monster while a cruciform tree of life rises above him.
Inside was the skeleton of a Maya high priest; he had been interred
with all his regalia and jewelry, and with a mosaic mask of jade
covering his face. Glyphs on the side of the sarcophagus date the
burial at about A.D. 700.

A somewhat similar burial has been found inside a pyramid at
Chichén Itzá in Yucatán, indicating that some pyramids at least
were built as tomb coverings. An interesting feature of some tombs
is the presence of a pipelinelike passage from the tomb to the sanc-

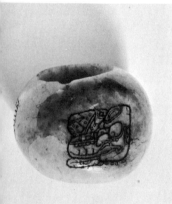

tuary, so that the deified spirit of the departed high priest could remain in contact with his successors.

The same style which the Maya sculptors evolved on a giant scale on their stelae and temple façades was followed on a miniature scale by the jade lapidaries. They now preferred apple-green and emerald-green stones to the blue-green and gray-green cherished by the Olmecs, and in their carving they used the greatest care to expose the very greenest layers of the stone. This produced plaques of eccentric shapes and uneven, rolling surfaces, to which the design was ingeniously adapted. Some Maya jades suffer from the *horror vacui* of their designers, who seem to have felt compelled to fill every available millimeter of space with forms and designs. But in the greatest of the Maya jades, such as the famous plaque found at Nebaj in the Guatemala highlands, this failing is offset by the elegance of the design and the powerful, dramatic movement of the principal personage depicted. To carve the extremely hard jade, Maya lapidaries used string saws, bird-bone drills and powdered jade for polishing. The great center of the craft appears to have been located in the Alta Vera Paz region of the Guatemala highlands, near the southern limit of the sphere of Maya influence. From there, Maya jades were exported to cities all over Mexico, as far north as Teotihuacán.

The Maya's brilliant technical proficiency appears also in their carving of shell and bone. It is beautifully demonstrated by a superbly and intricately carved, two-inch-high bone figurine from Chiapas. This little masterpiece is exhibited in the National Museum in Mexico City next to a six-foot photographic enlargement. It documents beyond words the absolute mastery of the ancient artists and the monumentality they were able to achieve regardless of scale.

There is almost no area of aesthetic expression in which the Maya did not excel. Their modeling in clay reached high levels of proficiency in such objects as the great urns and incense burners found at Palenque—huge vertical tubes, whose form is submerged in the applied decoration representing deities and dignitaries, surrounded by scrolls, masks and symbols of divine attributes and earthly power. But it is on the small island of Jaina, off the west coast of Campeche, that the most exquisite clay figurines of ancient America have been found. The island was the site of one of the many temple-cities which flourished all through the Maya area in Classic times. It was distinguished by the elaborate and well-preserved burial offerings that were made in the form of clay figurines.

The Jaina figurines are generally quite small, ranging from five to ten inches in height, and are delicately modeled of fine clay and brilliantly painted with red, yellow, white, green, black and Maya-blue (manganese) colors. Despite their small size, they are monumental in concept and majestic in appearance, splendid examples of the Maya ideal in the personages they represent. These include gorgeously dressed dignitaries, standing, or seated cross-legged; warriors with shields and weapons; and women with elaborate hairdresses and necklaces, the high social position of their sex documented by the fact that about one half of all known

Jaina figurines are female. Other representations are bearded old men, mothers and children, dwarfs and hunchbacks, and all the animals they knew—jaguars, armadillos, monkeys, rabbits, turtles, dogs, turkeys, crayfish, dolphins and owls and other birds. Some of the figurines are hollow and are filled with pebbles so that they rattle, while many others have whistles imbedded in the head or body, like the figurines found in Veracruz. Clay molds were introduced during the Classic Period; and many of the later figurines were mass-produced, the front being cast in a mold and the back filled in by hand. The quality of the mold-made figurines, however, was almost invariably lower, and the finest examples continued to be modeled entirely by hand.

Few Maya murals have survived the ravages of time, but in 1947 a spectacular discovery was made in the deep, unexplored jungles of Chiapas, where the Maya-descended Lacandon Indians still live their archaic life, hardly touched by modern Mexico. An American archaeologist, Giles G. Healy, who lived among the Lacandon and won their confidence, was taken to see the ruins they had so jealously guarded through the centuries: a small temple-city deeply hidden in the dense forest, one of whose buildings consisted of three chambers with high, vaulted ceilings, all of them entirely covered with the most extraordinary pre-Columbian murals yet found. Archaeologists have named the city Bonampak, meaning "painted walls" in Mayan.

The theme of the murals in each chamber is different. Those of the left chamber show rows of richly dressed personages attended by servants who carry great plumed fans on tall poles as symbols of their masters' dignity. Musicians play a great drum, long fantastic trumpets, rattles, whistles and turtle-shell rasps. A group of performers disguised as crabs, iguanas, alligators and other, imaginary animals perform a dance. On another side, several women are grouped about a throne, and in the place of honor a child is shown being presented to a group of dignitaries. On the ceiling are eight huge masks of the rain god Chac, shown both full face and in profile.

The murals of the chamber on the right show a great festival taking place on a ceremonial stairway where a group wearing enormous feather headdresses dance around three men performing a human sacrifice. Again the ceilings are decorated with masks of the rain god.

The middle chamber's murals show a fierce battle between richly ornamented Maya warriors and poorly dressed or nude opponents. Some panels show huge, complex battle scenes, full of intertwined struggling bodies in dramatic positions. Others show the triumphant Maya with their prisoners at their feet; one captive is sprawled dying across some steps in a pose reminiscent of Michelangelo. These frescoes are a unique triumph of dramatic, realistic composition unprecedented in an art which was generally stiffened by hieratic rules. They are also of great importance historically, for they show clearly how, toward the end of the long, peaceful Classic Period—the murals have been reliably dated at

about A.D. 800—militarism and the glorification of the warrior begins also among the Maya. The need for a growing military establishment may well have been dictated by just such events as the Bonampak murals illustrate—the attempted invasion of Maya lands by more primitive peoples, who had been dislocated and were being pressed upon by the great upheavals and migrations that followed in the wake of the fall of Teotihuacán. It is important to note, too, that Bonampak is one of the westernmost of the Maya cities, where such foreign incursions would be felt first.

A replica of the three chambers—with painstaking reconstructions of their superb frescoes—is exhibited in the great Maya Hall of the National Museum in Mexico City. The murals have also been reproduced in detail in special volumes published for UNESCO, and by the Carnegie Institution of Washington, under whose auspices so much significant pioneering work on the Maya has been done.

Very few other Maya murals have survived, and none of the scope of those of Bonampak. But this is compensated for, to some degree, by the glorious array of polychrome vases and plates painted in the mural manner. The vases follow the form of straight-sided beakers. They are rather small, rarely more than nine or ten inches high, while the plates are as large as fifteen inches in diameter. On a brightly burnished background of orange-red or orange-buff, the Maya artists painted great ceremonial scenes showing magnificently garbed priests with their attendants in the performance of sacred rituals, always accompanied by the elegant calligraphy of glyphs which told of the dates and constellations that marked the event. The great round plates, on the other hand, show more mundane aspects of life in their realistic portrayal of animals or—as on a famous tripod plate from Uaxactún —of a dancer in a stylized position drawn with a freedom and immediacy reminiscent of the great Japanese masters of the nineteenth century. Unfortunately, this plate, like so many others, suffers from having been ritually "killed" by having a hole punched through its center before being placed as an offering in the tomb, where it was then preserved from further destruction through the centuries.

Another form of decoration used by the Maya on pottery vessels is deep carving, giving a bas-relief effect very much like that found on the great stone monuments. The best of these are brilliantly incised and, in the strong Mexican sun, present a dramatic chiaroscuro effect. Toward the latter part of the Classic Period, a mass-production technique was developed in which clay molds impressed the design into panels on the bowl while the clay was still wet. Inevitably this produced rather shallow relief and less fine results.

The Maya also used a type of ware known as "thin orange," which is particularly dear to archaeologists because of the technical accomplishment of its fine, thin walls and because it is such a useful "index fossil." It was manufactured only during a short period at a center in the Puebla area of central Mexico and was ex-

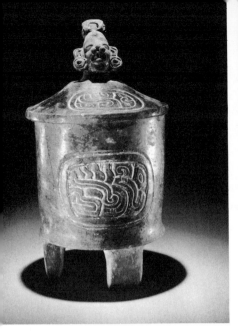

ported from there to such far-apart cities as Teotihuacán, Monte Albán, and Kaminaljuyú in the Guatemala highlands. Archaeologists are helped in dating specific sites and documenting trade connections when they find this ware buried with local types of pottery, artifacts and buildings. An odd Maya specialty was the shaping and flaking of eccentric flints and obsidians into fantastic forms. The material used was the stuff out of which knife blades, tools and weapons had been made since time immemorial, but these eccentric flints are formed into such delicate, fragile shapes that they could not have been made for any practical purpose. Groups of them are often found together in votive caches, sometimes as offerings below a great stone stele.

The pantheon of gods to whom the Maya dedicated all of their art and monuments was similar to that of the other cultures of the Classic Period, although somewhat more elaborate. They worshiped the gods of the rain, called Chacs, who sprinkled the earth with water from gourds to give men rain. But when angry, the Chacs could also empty their gourds all at once, causing devastating floods, or throw stone axes that became thunderbolts. The Maya also knew the jaguar god of the interior of the earth—possibly an Olmec heritage—and they had four very important gods of the cardinal points: the Itzamna, two-headed dragon serpents, each of whom ruled one of the four points of the compass and to whom were dedicated the chief colors, red, yellow, black and white. There were also gods of the sky, the sun, the moon and Venus, of the winds, the underworld, and of each segment of the calendar. The most appealingly depicted god is the young god of maize, whose images often show the same exquisite sensitivity and complete sculptural mastery that are shown by the stucco heads from the tomb at Palenque. What makes the personality of the Maya gods so particularly difficult to understand is that each had a dual aspect of good and evil. The dominance of the one or the other aspect could be predicted through the courses of the stars and are carefully recorded in the ritual calendar that guided the life of the Maya.

Our key to an understanding of the Maya pantheon and calendar was provided by the Franciscan missionary Diego de Landa, first Bishop of Yucatán, who in 1556 wrote the *Relación de las cosas de Yucatán*. This is the closest thing to a Rosetta stone for the reading of the Maya calendar glyphs. It contains a veritable mine of details about their customs, history and religion. The information he provides is rounded out for us by Indian accounts written immediately after the Conquest by the surviving sages in various towns. These are known as the *Books of Chilam Balam*, and the famous *Book of Books of Popul Vuh* of the Quiché Indians of the Guatemala highlands.

Only three of the Maya's own books have survived the book-burning organized by this same Bishop Landa. They include the Dresden Codex which is preserved in that East German city. It is a faithful copy of an even earlier manuscript dating from the height of the Classic Period. Artistically it is the most beautiful of the Maya codices, and it contains highly accurate mathematical and astronomical tables showing the divinities under whose aspect and protection each time segment fell. The Codex Peresianus in the Bibliothèque Nationale in Paris consists of a series of prophecies based on the twenty-year *katun* cycle and the twenty-times-twenty-year *baktun*. It dates from the period of decline at the end of the Classic Period. Poorly preserved, it was found in 1887 in the Paris library at the bottom of a pile of waste paper with a wrapper on which was written in a sixteenth-century hand the name Perez, from which its name is derived. The Codex Tro-Cortesianos in Madrid is the longest of the three codices and consists entirely of ritual rules and prescriptions for observances. It too is a copy of a Classic Period manuscript, but rather rudely and cursorily copied, as if it were made not by a trained artist but by a priest who needed a copy of the original book for personal use and purely practical purposes. For unknown reasons, this codex was cut into two parts, one of which was known as the Codex Cortesianos, the other as the Codex Troana, from which was coined the name Codex Tro-Cortesianos.

The pictorial style of the Maya codices closely parallels that of the painted vases, except that the personages shown represent gods rather than their earthly representatives, the priests, and that the glyphic calligraphy inevitably dominates the design of each of the folding pages, which follow one another like a folding screen.

Splendid painters and sculptors as they were, the Maya were architects par excellence. Their greatest triumphs were their splendid temple-cities, great ceremonial centers of breathtaking stuccoed pyramids, plazas and temples, where the people of an entire region assembled to participate in grand religious festivals, markets and civic ceremonies. Wide paved roads that survive to this day connected many of the temple-cities with each other, and encouraged active trade and mass pilgrimages. Their architects learned how to build stone bridges and even provided for such personal comforts as steam baths. But, most of all, they built for the greater glory of their gods. Their sanctuaries were covered with an architectural device which was exclusive to the Maya in the New World: the corbeled, or false, arch. (Somehow, the Maya never grasped the principle of the true, self-supporting stress arch.) The sanctuary, a small room, was a consecrated area and, presumably, it could be entered only by priests. It was marked with a high stone comb on its roof, so that it could be seen from

afar. The greater public ceremonies probably took place on the steep stone steps leading up to the sanctuary, where they could be witnessed by the massed people in the paved plaza below.

Each of the Maya cities had its own personal character and style, which is readily apparent in its sculpture and architecture. Some cities developed artists of great originality and daring, while other cities, perhaps poorer in resources, were content to remain imitators and followers. Some cities were frankly provincial, while others shone forth in regal splendor.

Among the greatest of the Maya cities was Tikal, deep in the lowland jungles of Petén, in northern Guatemala. Excavations made here by the University of Pennsylvania over the past few years have resulted in the most spectacular discoveries. This enormous city, which was able to house as many as 100,000 people at one time during great festivals, boasts temples as tall as modern twenty-two-story buildings. Charming human insights are found on the stuccoed walls of rooms in the residential palaces of Tikal, in the doodled graffiti probably drawn by young novices who lived here during their training for the priesthood. They show the same frank and irreverent spirit that was seen in the little incised designs on the ceremonial plaza bricks excavated by Gordon Ekholm at Comalcalco, Tabasco, in 1958.

The highest achievements of Maya sculpture were those of Palenque, in Mexico; of Yaxchilán and Piedras Negras on the Usumacinta river, between Mexico and Guatemala; and of distant Copán in Honduras, near the eastern frontier of the Maya area. Yaxchilán specialized in carved stone lintels spanning exterior doorways, and Piedras Negras developed a special form of stelae with deep niches containing sculptures of gods seated in Buddha-like positions. Copán, in a pleasant valley some two thousand feet above sea level, seems to have been one of the great intellectual centers of the Maya world. Here were solved many of the astronomical problems pertaining to the exact length of the tropical year; the most accurate tables of eclipses are found engraved here. The astronomical congress held here, and the unique quality of the stelae of Copán, have already been remarked upon. The architectural complex of Copán consists of a series of terraces and courts closely adjoining one another and connected with wide terracelike stairs; it is a closely built, compact center, which was revealed when the Rio Copán cut a new bed and washed through the ruins.

In the Guatemala lowlands, Quiriguá is famous for its colossal altars carved out of boulders weighing as much as fifty tons, in the shape of a mythic jaguar earth monster out of whose nichelike mouth emerges a human figure. This repeats an Olmec theme found at La Venta—men emerging from niches in jaguar-shaped altars. The most important of the altars at Quiriguá is known by the archaeological title of "Zoomorph P"; it shows the richly dressed figure of a young man sitting cross-legged inside the jaws of the great monster. One of the masterpieces of Maya sculpture, it is dated as of about A.D. 800.

At this time the cities of the Yucatán peninsula specialized in

the building of huge palaces and residential buildings with as many as a hundred rooms. At Sayil such a palace was built three stories high, the second and third stories set back so that the rooms of each floor came out on a wide terrace, connected by a great central staircase. At Uxmal there is another building in the same style, called Puuc. It is known as the "Nunnery," because its four sides form a perfect quadrangle, like a cloister garth, which is entered through a vaulted passageway. The first modern American to see it, John Lloyd Stephens, wrote this description in 1843: "We enter a noble courtyard, with four great façades looking down upon it, each ornamented from one end to the other with the richest and most intricate carving known in the art of the buildings of Uxmal; presenting a scene of strange magnificence, surpassing any that is now to be seen among its ruins." The ornaments Stephens comments upon are a characteristic of the Puuc style—in the massive concrete walls, thin, beautifully cut stones applied like tiles imbedded in cement. The decorations represent huge masks of the snout-faced rain gods, one placed above another in emphatic repetition, until their images filled entire façades.

The Puuc style is a development of the end of the Classic Period and has in it something of the overelaborateness which tends to announce the decadence of an art form and a culture. An interesting expression of the spirit of this late period is found in the tall masonry towers erected at some of the smaller temple-cities in southern Yucatán, at Rio Bec and other sites. These towers, built like steep-pitched pyramids, are topped by miniature temples; they seem designed to create the false impression of great height and massive size.

The history of the Maya goes back beyond the dawn of history. The earliest traces are found in the Guatemala highlands and date from before 2000 b.c. to about 1500 b.c. Known as Las Charcas, this culture produced simple pottery and the kind of small clay votive figurines typical of the Preclassic horizon all over Middle America. Many of them have a curiously Olmec quality about them, in their squat, compact form and facial expressions. A fasci-

nating form of stone sculpture also begins to be made at this time, tall stone mushrooms supported by crouching men. These are believed to represent the sacred, trance-inducing mushrooms still used in rituals by Indian magicians and *curanderos* (healers) in remote mountain valleys.

The important divisions of Maya history have been given names taken from the preamble of the *Book of Popul Vuh*. Mamóm ("Grandmother") refers to the Preclassic Period, Chicanel ("Concealer") to the transitional late Preclassic Period, Tzakol ("Builders") to the great Classic Period, and Tepeu ("Conquerors") to the late Classic Period.

The Mamóm Period extends from about 1500 B.C. to 500 B.C. and sees the continued use of small votive figurines, which now show

distinctly Maya physical features, and the use of finely burnished pottery. During the Chicanel Period, which covers the span between approximately 500 B.C. and A.D. 300, there is strong Olmec influence in such early monuments as the pyramid E-VII-Sub at Uaxactún. The calendar begins to be developed in slow stages, and many of the great temple-cities are founded in this period, although their great development will not occur until the next. During this period, too, an extraordinary cultural development took place in the Guatemala highlands which only recently has been recognized. Extremely elaborate stone altars and stelae have been found at Kaminaljuyú and other sites, indicating a highly developed culture as early as 500 B.C. Among the remarkable sculpture of this period are a stylized, silhouetted sculpture in the Museum of the American Indian, in New York, and a dramatic fragment showing an elaborately dressed priest holding two heads —now in the University Museum, in Philadelphia—and a great stele in the National Museum, in Guatemala City. Just how this culture fits into the panorama of Middle American civilization is still far from clear. How many of our present notions of historical development will be upset once we know more about this culture cannot be predicted. Like the question of the origin of the Olmecs, it is one of the many intriguing puzzles which are still to be solved by archaeology and which lend so much excitement and interest to this calm and sometimes rather plodding science.

The Tzakol Period, from about A.D. 300 to 650, saw the great flourishing of Maya art and architecture. Close contacts existed with Teotihuacán, whose cylindrical vase on rectangular feet was copied all over the Maya world. In return the Maya invented the corbeled arch and developed their mathematics and their calendar, all of which were borrowed by their neighbors in Oaxaca and Veracruz. The great temple-cities now began to take shape, and the first dates were recorded in stone (although it is likely that still earlier dates were recorded on wooden monuments which have disintegrated).

The Tzakol Period and the one following it, Tepeu, were called the "Old Empire" by the early Maya scholars to distinguish it from the very different later Maya-Toltec Period referred to as the "New Empire." These terms have long since been abandoned, although one still comes across them in earlier books and labels.

Tepeu, the last phase of the Classic Period, is marked by an increasing elaboration of style, and a much stepped-up pace of construction. This resulted in a proliferation of monuments, which climaxed in the last period just before the collapse of Classic Maya civilization. Tepeu is dated from about A.D. 650 until well into the tenth century, when the last Maya city ceased all artistic activity.

The collapse was so sudden that much work was simply left uncompleted. Pyramids were left uncrowned by temples; at Uaxactún the walls of the last building are unfinished. The end did not come everywhere at the same time, but seems to have spread from city to city like an infectious disease. Palenque, exposed on the western borders of the Maya world, was one of the first to be struck, and dated monuments ceased to be erected here after A.D. 784. Copán in the east came next, and the last monument is dated A.D. 800. Then follow in rapid order Quiriguá, Piedras Negras and Etzna after A.D. 810, and Tikal and Seibal dedicate their last monuments in A.D. 869, while Uaxactún and Chichén Itzá hang on until A.D. 889. The last Maya stele was erected in the unimportant small temple-city of La Muneca in Campeche in A.D. 909.

THE HUAXTECS

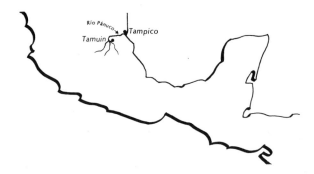

IN VERY EARLY TIMES THE MAYA ancestors of the Classic Period occupied the whole wide arc of the Gulf Coast of Mexico. Sometime
before 500 B.C., however, an intrusion of a new people into Veracruz cut off the Maya who lived on the northern reaches of the
Gulf Coast and left them in comparative isolation from the main
stream of Middle America's turbulent history. These northern
cousins of the Maya are the Huaxtecs. Although they continued to
speak a Maya language, they produced their own distinct art style,
whose continuous, uninterrupted development over a period of two
thousand years is unique in pre-Columbian history.

The area occupied by the Huaxtecs centered on the valley of the
Río Pánuco to the west of the Gulf port of Tampico and spread over
much of northern Veracruz and the bordering state of Tamaulipas.
Huaxtec sites in the Río Pánuco valley have been excavated chiefly
by the American archaeologists Gordon F. Ekholm and Richard S.
MacNeish. Six distinct stylistic periods have been analyzed, known
as Pánuco I to VI. The first two periods fall in the Preclassic horizon and are represented by characteristic votive clay figurines,

generally rather crudely made. During Pánuco III, from about A.D. 200 to 700—contemporary with Teotihuacán—the clay figurines became more elongated and graceful, often representing dancers with delicately defined details of dress, shoes, bracelets, necklaces and hairdresses. In contrast, their facial traits continued to follow the standardized stylization of archaic tradition. Pánuco IV, from about A.D. 700 to 1000, saw the introduction of clay molds, probably from Teotihuacán, for the making of figures. This resulted in the usual weakening of sculptural form and loss of individual character.

Periods V and VI belong to the Historic horizon and show some Toltec and Mixtec stylistic influences. This is especially evident in the famous frescoed frieze found at Tamuin on the Rio Pánuco, where an assemblage of gods, or priests disguised as gods, march in splendid procession, painted in a style related to the Mixtec codices. A unique Huaxtec form of this time is the spouted effigy vessel decorated with intricate designs applied with black paint on an eggshell-white background. Many of them have a wide, flaring form reminiscent of teapots, complete with spouts and handles, and are sometimes referred to as the "samovar type." Another Huaxtec specialty was the carving of ornaments of shell, decorated with busy, compact incised designs. These often include representations of the god Quetzalcóatl, who played so important a role in Huaxtec worship that it has been suggested that worship of this deity originated here.

But it is in stone sculpture that Huaxtec art reached its highest form of expression and made its most dramatic contribution. Characteristic are large stone figures carved in a severe, hieratic style. These usually represent female deities, who are shown standing with flexed arms and a nude upper torso, wearing a flaring skirt and a tall conical headdress with a shieldlike fan rising behind it. Their bodies are adapted to the geometric exigencies of the great stone slabs out of which they were carved. Only the face and headdress are sculptured fully in the round, the rest being carved only in light relief out of the massive stone. Their spirit reveals an affin-

ity with Toltec sculpture, although their faces are often more sensitive and expressive than those generally found on Toltec statues. At the bottom they usually have a rough-hewn tapered wedge forming a peg base, which was sunk into a wooden stand or base. A figure unique to Huaxtec sculpture is that of a grinning, bent old man, leaning heavily on a stick. The composition of these figures generally forms a harp-shaped loop and has the typical Huaxtec peg base.

The climax of Huaxtec sculpture consists of the large, lifelike stone figures carved fully in the round, of which the most famous example is the "Adolescent Boy." It is sculptured with superb realism and yet radiates a powerful, hieratic presence, reminiscent of great Egyptian Pharaonic figures. The "Adolescent Boy" represents a naked young man; large parts of his body are covered with tattoos of a form similar in detail to the Tamuin frieze and Huaxtec shell carvings, and he is carrying an infant on his back. This symbolism seems to be related to that found on other, possibly earlier Huaxtec stone figures, which are shown carrying a skeleton on their back. They have been interpreted as representing the concept of a man being transfigured into a god.

It is likely that future exploration in the Huaxteca will see many more ancient sites and objects brought to light. Through their study it may be possible to unravel the highly complex interrelationship of the Huaxtecs with the highland cultures and to throw light on the problems of their origin and their transmission of styles.

THE FALL OF THE THEOCRACIES

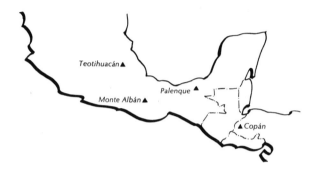

THE FALL OF TEOTIHUACÁN in the middle of the seventh century was the first evidence of the deep crisis which shook Middle America from one end to the other and brought to a bitter and violent end the glory of the Classic age. Within a hundred years Monte Albán and many other, smaller centers were being abandoned. The fabulous Maya cities flourished for another hundred and fifty or two hundred years and even reached new peaks of achievement in this period, but the same fatal sickness destroyed them all, one after another.

Many explanations have been offered as to the cause of this collapse. Soil exhaustion, massive deforestation of the highland valleys, droughts and resulting famines and epidemics, all have been put forward as the underlying cause of the disintegration of the great city-states. There is no doubt that in the highlands there was serious destruction of timberlands, and this may have produced local climatic changes. There had been an extraordinary consumption of wood—for the construction of the massive temple-cities; as fuel for the feeding of large new populations; and for burning the staggering amount of lime needed for the stuccoing of the hundreds of new pyramids, temples and palaces. The Indian agricultural technique—clearing the land by burning, cultivating the soil without allowing for its replenishment, thus hastening its exhaustion, and then abandoning it—was equally destructive; it almost certainly resulted in periodic famine and in widespread epidemics, and these must have undermined popular faith in the divine power of priests, whose fervent propitiations and costly sacrifices had failed to avert disaster.

Revolts of the increasingly oppressed peasants against their priestly rulers have been suggested, and impressive evidence of this is seen in the innumerable smashed portraits of priests found in the ruins of Maya cities. Again and again, on altars and stelae, the faces of priestly figures are brutally violated, while those of the gods who hover above and crouch below them are undamaged. At Piedras Negras, in a splendid work depicting a court ceremony, the face of every one of the high dignitaries was destroyed, but the figures of the gods on the nearby stelae were not so much as scratched. It was as if the despoilers of the city had vented their anger on the priests and had carefully avoided any show of disrespect to the gods. They destroyed the symbolic seat of power and the mark of their oppression, somewhat as the citizens of Paris were to do when they pulled down the Bastille a thousand years later.

When we consider the centuries-long continuity of power implied by the creation of those vast stone cities, we can presume that local or secondary causes—such as an isolated revolt of peasants or an epidemic of drought and famine—could not have caused so many powerful city-states to be destroyed, or such a vast system of theocratic rule to disappear. As the Mexican archaeologist Ignacio Bernal first pointed out, the root cause must have been inherent in the fabric of theocratic thought and society itself.

In the beginning, the young theocracies gave an enormous impetus to civilization and accomplished almost miraculous achievements with primitive tools and despite the lack of the large domestic animals that were the basis of European and Asiatic life —the horse, the cow, the sheep and the pig. The priests of the late Preclassic and early Classic Periods so organized their village society as to provide a surplus of food and of energy; and this made possible the construction of the first great pyramids and temples, and the expansion of these centers of worship into true cities. The new society, thus organized, permitted the specialization of work, and this in turn provided the skills and talent which produced the glorious achievements of their golden age—in architecture, painting, sculpture, astronomy, writing, mathematics, pottery and weaving.

Once the theocratic system had established itself, however, later generations of priests accepted their inherited power as a natural if not divinely ordained state of things and thought only of conserving their gains. The priestly elite grew in numbers and in demands, increasingly separated from the people by caste consciousness. The enormous palaces built during the late Classic Period in the Maya cities are evidence that an oppressively large aristocracy of priests and administrators developed, perhaps multiplying by the same mathematical progression as that which C. Northcote Parkinson, in *Parkinson's Law*, has so penetratingly observed in our modern bureaucracy. In time, theocratic society became fossilized and lost its interior energy and power. The creative social impulse declined, and the fabric of society was weakened by new pressures. These include discontent of the masses and possibly famines, but also the relentless push of barbarians from without and the rise of a new social group within—the warrior class—perhaps called into being by the priestly rulers in response to the new threats. With the warriors came the first signs of a new philosophy which exalted power, a philosophy which was to dominate the next period.

The combination of strains on the weakened theocratic city-states brought about their downfall, perhaps with different combinations of factors in each instance, but with the same destructive result. Chaos followed, and for centuries culture continued on a poor and low level in the same regions where high civilization once reigned. Finally, a new civilization gestated and new peoples emerged to produce new forms of art. But the new military empires, founded on force and sustained by tribute, never established the peace or reached the splendor and dignity of their ancestors.

THE LAST OUTPOSTS

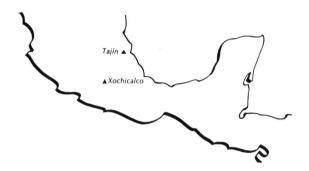

AFTER THE FALL OF TEOTIHUACÁN, a desolate void existed in the Valley of Mexico. The life of high culture was carried on only in a few small, unimportant centers along the southern rim of the valley; and until the founding of Tula by the Toltecs, some three centuries later, there was no new focus of civilization to replace the destroyed metropolis. One by one the other great Classic cities fell. The lamps were kept burning in only two important centers which survived into the new Historic age of military kingdoms. They were the great temple cities of Tajín, in northern Veracruz, and Xochicalco, the place of flowers, in the beautiful Valley of Morelos, near Cuernavaca.

Both of these centers have their origins in Early Classic times, but they experience their most vigorous expansion during this Late Classic Period. The brutal new concepts of the invading barbarians make their effects felt even here. The people of Xochicalco—whose great sanctuary dedicated to Quetzalcóatl was strategically located on a terraced mountaintop—found it necessary to construct a powerful military fortress on another mountain nearby. This was large enough for all the neighboring population to take refuge in when threatened by what must have been repeated attacks on their rich and fruitful valley. Though they worshiped a peaceful god, they lived always under the threat of sudden violence.

At Tajín, on the other hand, the fierce and bloodthirsty rituals which mar the next period were already being practiced, albeit on a smaller scale. Bas-relief murals now show ferocious eagles—the animal disguise or impersonation of the sun—who dive from the sky to carry back the sacrificed hearts of men. The repeated representations of human skulls are the first indications of the incipient necrophilia which was to reach such an extravagant climax under the Aztecs. Even the ancient ritual ball game became an occasion for sacrifice, and stone ball-court markers show players in full regalia decapitated in honor of the gods. Detailed sacrificial scenes too are shown in some of the reliefs of the great temples. The very

name of Tajín itself is evidence of the new spirit: it means thunder, and it indicates that the great temple was dedicated to the old rain god, now represented only by his fiercest aspect, thunder and lightning.

The arts, however, continued to flourish at Tajín. The same reliefs showing human sacrifices are decorated with flowing, almost lyrical meander scrolls in the best Classic taste, and their execution is flawless. The brutality of the subject is not yet reflected by the style. Architecture too reached new heights. Splendid temples, courts, terraces, pyramids and as many as six new ball courts testify to the energy and vitality of the time.

The great central pyramid is the most important architectural monument on the Gulf Coast. It was built with six recessed levels. The façade of each level is lined with a row of deep niches, 367 in all, which give the pyramid a unique light-and-dark aspect reminiscent in its mystery of the façade of a Gothic cathedral. The entire surface was originally covered with a heavy coat of burnished, painted stucco, which must have been a gorgeous sight in the bright light of the hot Mexican sun. The sanctuary on top was so well preserved that it could be completely reconstructed. Among the technical feats of Tajín's architects are great open windows and cement ceilings so solidly built that no beams or columns were needed to support their amazingly wide spans, one of which covers an area of nine by ten yards. Other elements were borrowed from the Maya, with whom they must have been in close contact: corbeled arches, stone roof combs on top of their temples, and glyph writing which closely follows the Maya pattern. Tajín continued to flourish into the Toltec period, and seems to have been finally abandoned only sometime after A.D. 1000, when the last new dawn of Indian art in the Valley of Mexico was about to break under the Aztecs.

At Xochicalco, the chief structure is distinguished by the superb bas-relief decorations that encircle its walls. They depict the great plumed serpent Quetzalcóatl—whose worship now centered here —and a series of splendidly caparisoned priests with huge, cascading headdresses of quetzal feathers, seated crosslegged, hands held in meaningful gestures and great speech scrolls ascending from their mouths. There is a surprising Maya flavor to these figures, evidence of strong Maya influence. One fascinating interpretation of the many majestic figures on the bas-reliefs suggests that the works commemorate a great gathering of the high priests of various cities of the highlands called to correct the calendar or to celebrate some great event such as the installation of a new supreme high priest of the cult of Quetzalcóatl. The glyph signs next to each priest seem to represent different cities, some of which have been fully identified.

The sages of Xochicalco kept alive the civilized heritage of the splendid Classic Period through the long centuries of decline and barbarism in the other highland valleys. Their ultimate triumph was in their ability to bequeath their arts, their technical achievements, and to some degree their religion, to the new people who finally came to dominate the highland valleys, the Toltecs. The ascendancy of this people was climaxed in the tenth century during the life of the greatest Mexican culture hero, the historic Quetzalcóatl, a high priest, reared and educated in this tradition, who went on to become king of the warrior Toltecs. His life and career dramatize the absorption by the vigorous but still half-nomadic Toltecs of the ancient culture of the highlands. But his story and that of his people belong to another chapter.

THE TOLTECS

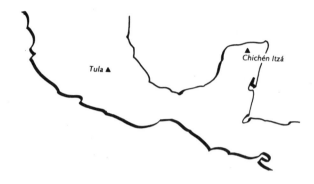

IN THE BEGINNING OF THE TENTH CENTURY new hordes of invaders swept down into the Valley of Mexico from the northwestern regions of Mexico. They were headed by a great chieftain named Mixcóatl, a kind of Indian Genghis Khan, who must have been possessed of extraordinarily dynamic personal qualities. He is the first historic personage we meet in Middle American history.

Within a few years Mixcóatl conquered the Valley of Mexico. He selected as the site for his new capital a place called Culhuacán, strategically situated on a small peninsula jutting into the central lake, at the foot of an easily defended, cave-studded mountain known today as the Cerro de la Estrella, the Hill of the Star. Curiously, this first Toltec city was also the only one to survive the disaster that was to strike their empire three hundred years hence, and the only one whose dynasty continued until the Spanish conquest.

During a military expedition into the Valley of Morelos, Mixcóatl met and married the Princess Chimalma, a daughter of the Huitznahuacanos, the surviving old aristocracy of theocratic times.

But in 947 Mixcóatl was assassinated by a rival contender for his throne. A few months afterward his posthumous son was born. Chimalma herself died in childbirth, and the orphaned heir was given the name Ce Acatl Topíltzin, One Reed, Our Prince, after the calendrical sign that ruled the year of his birth. He was reared by his maternal grandparents, who probably lived in the fabled, magnificently situated city of Tepotzlán. In this region, affiliated with Xochicalco, the Classic religion was still maintained and the little prince grew up in the old faith. He became a priest and in time, aided by his personal brilliance and the prestige of his parentage, was elevated to the high priesthood of the cult of the god Quetzalcóatl, the Plumed Serpent. According to immemorial custom he then assumed the name of the god whose living incarnation he was considered to be, and was known thenceforward as Quetzalcóatl Topíltzin, or more briefly, simply as Quetzalcóatl. This caused endless confusion to the Spanish chroniclers and historians since then, who have hopelessly mixed up the god, the historic personage and the other high priests who all through Indian history have borne the divine title.

The priest-prince Quetzalcóatl now became the protagonist of a legitimist political movement in the Toltec capital at Culhuacán. He traveled to the Valley of Mexico and at once undertook a search for the bones of his father, Mixcóatl, whose remains he found and interred on the Cerro de la Estrella. He then declared his father a deity; as the Cloud Serpent, god of stars and numbers, the father remained a member of the pantheon from that time on. Indian history records that a temple was built over Mixcóatl's tomb, although its remains, unfortunately, have not been found. Quetzalcóatl was attacked on this same mountain by the usurper of his father's throne, but Quetzalcóatl slew him on the summit of the mountain after a decisive victory which established Quetzalcóatl as the undisputed chief of the Toltecs. For reasons not clear to us, he immediately decided to move the capital. After various peregrinations, he finally selected a place near the northern frontier of his realm, Tula, and in 980 he began to build a grandiose metropolis,

which was to be the climax and the confirmation of his civilizing mission among the still half-barbaric people of his father.

Tula was settled by Toltecs and large groups deriving from the old population of the valley. Among these were the Amanteca, a caste of artists and craftsmen descended from the last survivors of Teotihuacán, who were brought here by Quetzalcóatl to help in the construction of Tula. Quetzalcóatl's reign lasted for only nineteen years, but later legends attribute to him not only the city of Tula but all of the benefits of civilization. Toltec traditions credit him with the discovery of corn, which he was said to have stolen from the old and jealous god of the infernos; with the invention of the ritual calendar and the art of divining good and evil omens; with writing, painting, medicine, astrology; in short, with all of the advances and inventions of the Classic age. In this way the legends symbolically document the absorption of the ancient civilization of the highlands by the nomadic Toltecs under the aegis of Quetzalcóatl, whose own birth is symbolic of the merging of the newcomers with the old population.

Out of the barbaric wilderness the Toltecs had brought with them the cult of their terrible tribal god of war, the bloodthirsty Tezcatlipoca ("Smoking Mirror"), who demanded human sacrifices. Quetzalcóatl, however, preached the much more humane religion of his mother's people, derived from Classic times. He insisted that his god desired them to make no sacrifices except snakes and butterflies. His prayer even contained the germ of monotheism: "We adore one sole lord whom we hold as god. . . ." But his spirit was too far advanced for his time, and he incurred the unforgiving enmity of the priests of Tezcatlipoca. They intrigued against him unceasingly, and in 999 they forced him to flee from Tula. The legends speak of a struggle between him and the irresistible evil magic of his rival, the high priest of Tezcatlipoca. This has been interpreted as a struggle for power between the old priestly caste, represented by Quetzalcóatl, and the new military aristocracy, identified with the priests of the war god.

With a small group of followers, Quetzalcóatl started on an ad-

venturous migration, staying for a while in Cholula, then proceeding to the Gulf Coast. Here he set sail for the "Land of the Black and the Red," probably Yucatán, where he died. Before leaving, however, Quetzalcóatl swore to return one day from the east to redeem his throne and to reign once more in peace over his people. It was a fateful promise.

Quetzalcóatl is the most appealing personality in Indian history. He personified the heritage of the Classic Period, and the legends refer to his reign as the Golden Age. The forces which overthrew his rule and forced him into exile were the oppressive new militarism and its bloodthirsty religion. But, although they gained and kept power, a curious sense of guilt seems to have attached itself to their memory of Quetzalcóatl. Centuries later, the Aztecs ruled all of what had been the Toltec empire and considered themselves to be its rightful heirs. The proudest title of those later emperors was Lord of Culhuacán, the first and last Toltec city. With this title the Aztecs bolstered their claim to succession in the Toltec empire.

Although Quetzalcóatl himself was exiled from Tula, the civilizing of the once barbarian Toltecs continued without interruption. Within a short time, their parvenu empire usurped the cultural claims of ancient Teotihuacán. The very word *Toltec* came to mean "builder," and "man of culture and learning." The Aztecs attributed all of the achievements of the Classic Period to the Toltecs, and this invalid claim was believed until very recent years, when archaeologists conclusively disproved it. But a good many Teotihuacán stone masks are still mislabeled at Toltec in earlier literature and are so presented in some museum cases.

Like most of the great art styles of Middle America, Toltec art seems to appear suddenly, full-blown and without any early transitional forms to be found. Toltec sculpture introduces a new rigidity, a stiffness never encountered before, a perfect reflection of the military spirit of its time.

The most famous example of Toltec sculpture is the series of immense stone caryatids from the Temple of Quetzalcóatl at Tula. Although the temple was dedicated to this pacific deity, the monumental atlantean figures which support the temple roof represent Toltec warriors in full regalia and standing stiffly at attention. Over fifteen feet high, they are carved out of a series of cylindrical drums joined one to another with mortise and tenon. Their faces have the anonymous, vacant expression of well-drilled military automatons. Their chests are incongruously decorated with huge stylized butterfly pendants, symbols of Quetzalcóatl, and the stiff bristles of straight feathers which rise from their headbands lack the flowing grace of the quetzal feathers of an earlier, more elegant age. Altogether, they appear a bit stilted and awkward in their composition. Yet there is about them a vigor and a directness that are a refreshing relief after some of the flamboyance of the last decadence of Classic art. The best of Toltec stone sculpture also has an admirable structural simplicity, with an interesting adaptation

of natural forms to the basic cubes and cylinders of the great basalt blocks.

The heroes of this new age were soldiers, and the new temples were built for their active participation. To the small, exclusive sanctuary now were added grand vestibules and colonnades where the warriors assembled in splendid arrays to participate in the solemn rituals. Their stone personifications upheld the temple itself, while they themselves were called upon to provide the essential sacrifices for the new bloodthirsty gods—that is, to provide

human victims, and this they did by taking prisoners in their wars, which now became a steady occupation. The ancient Indian legends ascribe the very invention of war to Tezcatlipoca, for war was now no longer a question of raids and defense, or the result of greed and rapacity, but a ritual necessity and a religious prescription. Horrendous monuments rose next to their temples: *tzompantlis*, great racks on which were displayed the skulls of the captives who had been sacrificed to the gods. The base of the *tzompantli* generally was a low stone platform whose walls were decorated with bas-relief stone panels showing rows of skulls.

This period saw the introduction of the warrior orders of the eagle and the jaguar, two military organizations that have been compared to such medieval European knightly orders as the Knights Templar and the Teutonic Knights. They actually wore helmets in the shape of jaguar and eagle heads, and jaguar skins and eagle feathers. Their religious aspect is emphasized in the personification of the sun by the eagle and the earth by the jaguar. New bas-relief friezes, showing proud processions of jaguars and eagles, were carved on the walls of temples and pyramids. But, whereas the jaguars of Teotihuacán paced in pursuit of rain clouds, the eagles of these reliefs were devouring human hearts. And in the Temple of the Warriors in Chichén Itzá, Toltec frescoes celebrate a raid on an open city in preference to the rain god's paradise so lovingly shown in Teotihuacán's famous mural (see page 88).

One of the most successful sculptural forms developed by the Toltecs is the reclining figure of Chac-Mool, the messenger of the gods, who holds a bowl to receive offerings. Splendid stone figures of him are found in the important Toltec temples. Their newly rediscovered form served as inspiration for the English sculptor Henry Moore in his famous series of reclining personages.

Another effective Toltec innovation was the serpent columns upholding the great lintels across temple entrances—great stylized plumed serpents, their open jaws jutting forward to flank the temple doorway, their tails sweeping up in a rectangular S shape to support the lintel.

The architecture of the Toltecs is highly dramatic and theatrical. It was evidently very rapidly constructed to impress a great popu-

lace, rather than painstakingly built to last through the centuries. Poor techniques were used, with walls mostly of adobe and coarse stones. Virtually nothing has remained of the murals; they were destroyed by fire and by the crumbling of the ill-made walls. The stone bas-reliefs that have remained were originally brilliantly painted and must have been a stunning sight with their bright primary colors shimmering in the sunlight.

The Toltecs were least successful in their handling of clay. Their pottery is very simple and rarely much more than utilitarian. Its style, called Tula, is an early version of the forms later brought to perfection in Aztec times. It is, in fact, contemporary with the style sometimes labeled Aztec I, produced in the southeast of the Valley of Mexico, at Chalco, and in Puebla. Votive clay figurines were made, but in a degenerated form with little artistic effort. They were crudely made in molds, flat, solid rectangular little tablets of such very poor quality that they seem to have been made for peasants and the poorer levels of society—perhaps the descendants of the old inhabitants—rather than for the dominant elite. There were some efforts at ambitious, large-scale clay sculpture similar in conception to the life-size figurines of Remojadas, but much more crudely executed and less sensitive in expression. Huge clay braziers with the effigy of the rain god have also been found, as impressive in size as they are unattractive in design and workmanship. Some small counterparts of these braziers, however, probably intended for personal use, a tradition that goes back to Teotihuacán and beyond, are delightfully stylized and refreshingly direct. On the basic cylindrical shape of the vessel the features of the rain god were applied with little clay rolls—the huge goggle eyes, the twisted nose representing intertwined serpents, the mouth from which rain pours in whiskerlike stylization.

Few Toltec luxury objects, such as fine ware and precious-stone jewelry, have been found, possibly because they did not make elaborate tomb offerings, but more probably because the Spartan Toltecs had little taste for such things. It was in their time, however, that metallurgy was introduced into Mexico. From Costa Rica and Panama, and even from Peru, came gold objects and then the technique of casting gold and copper. But this fine craft became the specialty of the Toltecs' southern neighbors and contemporaries, the Mixtecs, who inhabited the highlands of Oaxaca and Puebla; from them the Toltecs imported, through trade and perhaps tribute, what luxury goods they used.

One very important type of commercial ware of this period is called *plumbate*, because of its metallic and often lead-colored sheen. It was produced in only one place, probably near the present border between Mexico and Guatemala, on the Pacific slope of the ancient rich region known as Soconusco, and the process by which

it was made seems to have been a closely guarded secret. Plumbate was very highly valued in its own time and was traded as far as Nayarit in the northwest and Panama to the south. It has a beautiful vitrified surface, of such extraordinary hardness that it can scarcely be scratched with steel. About half of the plumbate ware that has been found consists of effigy vessels of gods, men and animals, often of fine sculptural quality. Other vases are decorated with incised motifs frequently reminiscent of the Classic Scroll Style of Veracruz. Plumbate ware came in a wide range of colors, from lead gray to olive green, reddish brown and bright orange. Like fine orange ware, plumbate is especially useful to archaeologists in helping to place and date other objects found in association with it. It was made only during a relatively brief period, from shortly before A.D. 1000 to about A.D. 1200, when it ceased to be traded.

After the exile of Ce Acatl Quetzalcóatl there follows a dynasty of kings of Tula whose rhythmic names and individual dates are carefully recorded in the Indian codices—from Matlacxochitl, Nahuyotzin, Matlacotzin, Tlicoctzin to the last Toltec king, Huémac. They engaged in enormous campaigns of military expansion and sent expeditions as far as Nicaragua. They brought about the political unification of most of the highland valleys and established an enormously wide diffusion of their art style and the structure of their society based on a military aristocracy.

The Toltecs, shortly after the establishment of the capital at Tula, conquered northern Yucatán, beginning with the occupation of Chichén Itzá in A.D. 987. According to the Maya chronicles in the *Books of Chilam Balam*, Toltec invaders—whom the Maya called the Itzá—came from the southwest and conquered the ancient pilgrimage city of Chichén, on the great Cenote, or well of sacrifice; from then on the city was known as Chichén Itzá, "the city of the Itzá at the rim of the well." The chronicles record that the chieftain who led the Itzá was a high priest called Kukulcán, a literal Maya translation of Quetzalcóatl, or "plumed serpent." Unlike Ce Actl Quetzalcóatl of Toltec history, however, Kukulcán seems to have been a brutal, bloodthirsty and lecherous conqueror, far different from the noble culture hero who bore the same title. It is unlikely that the two traditions refer to the same individual, but it is important to remember that the *Books of Chilam Balam* were written by the descendants of the vanquished. Their memory of an enemy leader is inevitably far different from the image kept alive by his own people.

The Toltecs built a new city at Chichén Itzá that rivaled Tula; there occurred the most brilliant and elaborate flowering of their culture. Its architecture has amazingly many close parallels with that of Tula; at times it seems as if the same architects had built the temples of both cities. We see the same serpent columns, the same reclining figures of Chac-Mool, the same awful *tzompantlis*, or skull-rack platforms, and the same processions of jaguars and eagles in the bas-reliefs on the walls of temples. The Toltecs brought with them all their rituals and institutions, such as the worship of Venus, the morning and evening star which embodied the concept of duality. Venus was also believed to be the heavenly personification of Quetzalcóatl. The military orders of the jaguar and the eagle played a great role at Chichén Itzá. To them was dedicated a magnificent colonnade, some 425 feet long and 45 feet wide, upheld by five long lines of columns.

There is a marvelous sense of restrained power and purity of line in the buildings of Chichén Itzá, best exemplified perhaps by the temple-topped pyramid now called El Castillo. Some 180 feet square, the pyramid rises in nine terraced levels to a height of 75 feet, each side having a wide ceremonial staircase leading to the square, massive sanctuary on top. It is decorated with typical Toltec warrior figures sculptured on the jambs of the doorways and on the interior pillars that support the roof; its roof merlons are ornamented with stylized bisected conch shells, a favorite Toltec motif. The temple is an illuminating example of the use of significant and mystical numbers so often found in symbolic Indian architecture. Each stairway has ninety-one steps, which together with the last step of the upper platform add up to 365 steps, the number of days

in the solar calendar. A stairway divides each of the nine levels of the pyramid, giving a total of eighteen sections on each side, memorializing the eighteen months of the Maya year. Each side of the pyramid is decorated with fifty-two panels representing the fifty-two-year cycle of Venus, the basis of the ritual calendar of the Historic Period. The completion of each cycle was marked by solemn ceremonies and was celebrated by the ritual breaking of old pottery and utensils, and often by the construction of a new pyramid over the core of an earlier one.

That is what took place here. The pyramid of El Castillo was superimposed over a smaller, earlier edifice that dates from the first years of the Toltec conquest. This became clear when excavations were made in the floor of the temple in 1937, leading to the discovery of the completely intact superstructure of the old temple below. A splendid sculpture of a Chac-Mool was found in its antechamber, and in the inner sanctuary the now famous, mysteriously lifelike, red jaguar throne was discovered. This massive five-foot-long sculpture was carved out of a massive block of limestone, completely painted with brilliant vermilion cinnabar with inlaid white flint teeth and eyes made of two balls of apple-green jade. Some eighty jaguar skin spots placed all over the animal's body were made of jade disks the size of silver dollars. The throne appears to have been designed not for a man but for the sun. Resting on it was found a solar disk of wood covered with rich turquoise inlay, on top of which a small jade mask and a necklace of precious red shell had been placed as offerings.

The most dramatic feature of Chichén Itzá, and the reason for its importance in ancient times, is the great sacred well near which it was built. The solid limestone cover of northern Yucatán is not cut through by any rivers, but rain seeps through to an underground drainage system, which is hidden except in a few places where the limestone crust has caved in. These natural wells are known as cenotes; they were, and still are, the sole source of water throughout this region. The great Cenote at Chichén Itzá (there is also a smaller one which supplied the city with water) was considered sacred and was dedicated to the rain god. It is a huge gap in the ground some two hundred feet in diameter, with sheer walls that drop straight down to the water some sixty-five feet below the surface of the ground. Pilgrims came here from far-distant places, and sacrifices were thrown into the well from a small temple, whose ruins still stand at its edge.

In 1900 the American consul Edward H. Thompson (no relation to the contemporary Maya authority J. Eric S. Thompson) began to dredge the well. His sensational find included a great treasure of sacrificial objects of pottery, wood, alabaster, jade, rubber and, most important, copper and gold. These were analyzed in 1952 by Samuel K. Lothrop, who showed that most of the gold objects were imported from Panama and Costa Rica. Complete cast figurines and bells seem to have been favored trade objects, as were plain round gold disks which were then embossed and decorated locally.

These gold disks are much the most interesting of the Cenote finds and show in fine, ornate detail dramatic scenes of battle between victorious Toltecs and fleeing Maya. One depicts a naval battle. Others show Toltec warriors interrogating Maya prisoners, the surrender of vanquished Maya personages to Toltec chieftains, symbolic Toltec eagles attacking terrified Maya, portraits of sumptuously dressed Toltec notables, and—on the most famous of the disks—a resplendently attired Toltec warrior-priest, assisted by his acolytes, extracting the heart of a sacrificial Maya victim. These *repoussé* designs have a fluidity and a realistic style which suggest that they are the work of Maya artists in Toltec service—a suggestion that is strengthened by the clearly Maya style of the sky serpents observing the scenes from above, of the earth monsters crouching below, and of the Classic scroll-type motifs on the rims of the disks.

An interesting insight into the nature of Toltec rule in Yucatán is provided by the new words of Nahuatl derivation which now found their way into the language of the Maya. They include *tepal* (lord), *macehual* (the common people, plebeians), *tecpan* (a word which stands for the ruler's residence and also for the house where arms are stored), *tenamitl* (walled or fortified town, a new invention dating from this period) and *tepeu* (glory, the military grandeur of conquerors).

There is a crucial difference, however, between the history of Chichén Itzá and the history of the empire of the Mexican highland Toltecs. The Maya Toltecs, as some archaeologists like to call them, were rather quickly absorbed into the main stream of Maya life and art, and they soon disappeared virtually without a trace. Only the heritage of military organization survived them. Their name continued only in the claim to Toltec descent made by all the ruling houses of the city-states that vied for control of the Maya realm. But even they were Maya in heart and soul, and their claim to a Toltec heritage is rather like that of the English aristocracy to a Norman descent.

Tula, even though violently destroyed by new barbarian invaders, continued to exercise an enormous influence through all the rest of the highland history. The style of its architecture remained dominant, and its gods remained in the center of the pantheon. It also set a pattern of social and political development, of brilliant if short-lived military empires—a pattern which was to be repeated again and again, and whose brilliant last representatives were the Aztecs. In later legends and histories, the Toltecs appear as the great civilizing force, the embodiment of all virtues. The consciousness of their glory remained so strong that when, after the Conquest, the descendants of Moctezuma were offered a title by the Spaniards, they chose that of "Count Moctezuma of Tula" and returned to live in that ancient ruined city where a small Aztec settlement existed.

The exposed situation of Tula on the extreme northern frontier of civilization and the increasing tensions that divided its population caused a series of civil disturbances which forced the last Toltec king, Huemac, to abandon the city as his capital in 1168. He found refuge at Chapultepec, the hilltop site where centuries later the ill-fated Emperor Maximilian built his castle. There

Huemac died, in 1174—it is not clear whether by murder or suicide—after a reign of seventy years beset by endless troubles. The great Toltec empire now quickly split up into warring factions. Thereafter, the Valley of Mexico was torn by incessant hostilities until the unification achieved by the Aztecs in the beginning of the fifteenth century.

Tula itself survived until 1224, when it was invaded by northern barbarians. In its debilitated state it could no longer successfully resist. The city was devastated with unusual fury and put to the torch. The principal temples and palaces were razed; the towering columns and sculptured walls were deliberately leveled. They remained thus, accumulating a covering of debris and dust through the centuries, until they were re-erected by modern archaeology.

The fall of the Toltec empire seems to have been brought about by the usual combination of causes. There was an inner weakening of the fabric of society resulting in part from the fact that the later generations of the Toltecs, safely established at the summit of power, neglected to pursue economic necessities such as the growing of corn. Instead, they concentrated on exacting tribute from subject peoples—food and such luxuries as shimmering quetzal plumes and precious stones for personal adornment. The onset of droughts, famines and plagues, the discontent of subject peoples, internal religious strife, the growing power of jealous noble families ensconced in their own feudal domains—all these helped to undermine the central authority of the empire and weaken it in the face of increasingly strong attacks by the northern barbarians. As the attackers noticed that their sporadic, probing forays met with less determined, less effective resistance, they repeated their raids in larger numbers and more powerful formations. Finally, among the barbarians rose a great chief, the dread war lord Xólotl, and under his brilliant leadership they conquered all of the Valley of Mexico, just as the Toltecs under Mixcóatl had done, three centuries earlier.

THE POST-CLASSIC MAYA

To EXTEND THEIR POWER AND DOMAIN, the rulers of Chichén Itzá soon formed an alliance with another Toltec-dominated city, Mayapán. At first the old Maya city of Uxmal also participated, but it soon dropped out, and its place was taken by the Toltec city of Izamal, making the powerful triple alliance a purely Toltec affair. This alliance remained effective for some two hundred years, until about 1200, when increasing rivalries and tensions brought the ruling houses of the three cities into a series of internecine wars that ended with the hegemony of Mayapán.

One dominant personality stands out in this period, one of those remarkable individuals whose dynamic character and powerful achievements appear in sharp relief in the otherwise rather impersonal Indian legends and histories. He is Hunac Ceel, also called Cauich, and his first appearance on the stage of history was at the most dramatic possible moment—the offering of sacrifices to the rain gods at the well of Chichén Itzá. It was the custom at this time to throw living victims into the Cenote, and to retrieve one such victim in order to learn from him the rain god's message as to whether the coming year would be one of rain or of drought. On the occasion when Hunac Ceel was present, however, no victim survived to bring back the crucial message from the gods. The story of what happened next is related in the Maya *Books of Chilam Balam*, written at Chumayel after the Conquest (R. L. Roy's translation):

> Then those who were to be thrown arrived; then they began to throw them into the well that their prophecy might be heard by their rulers. Their prophecy did not come. It was Hunac Ceel, Cauich was the name of the man there, who put out his head at the opening of the well on the south side. [This is where the sacrificial temple's ruins still stand.] Then he began to take it. Then he came forth to declare the prophecy. Then began the taking of the prophecy. Then began his prophecy. Then they began to declare him ruler. Then he was set in the seat of the rulers by them. Then they began to declare him head chief. He was not the ruler formerly.

The accounts are somewhat unclear as to Hunac Ceel's actual rule, but he seems to have become the ruler of Mayapán and to have made this, his native city, the dominant city of the old triple alliance. War broke out when the ruler of Chichén Itzá, one Chac Xib Chac, stole the bride of Ah Ulil, the chief of the third allied city of Izamal, during the wedding ceremony. This Maya version of the ancient Helen of Troy theme led to a war by Mayapán and Izamal against the bride-stealing Chac Xib Chac of Chichén Itzá. He was defeated, and as the Maya book relates, he was "trampled upon." His followers were forced to flee Chichén Itzá, which then disappeared from history. Hardly was this conquest consummated, however, when Hunac Ceel turned on his erstwhile ally, the brideless Ah Ulil of Izamal, perhaps motivated by rivalry but in any case determined to eliminate all competition to Mayapán's hegemony. Hunac Ceel conquered once again. The books of Maya history record laconically that the sons of holy Izamal were given in tribute "to feed and nourish Hapay Can." This is a Maya deity whose name means sucking snake, and the statement leaves little doubt that Hunac Ceel's prisoners were sacrificed to gratify the gods.

Hunac Ceel extended Mayapán's rule over some dozen formerly independent city-states from which he exacted tribute. The sons of their ruling houses lived as hostages in Mayapán, living assurance of their continuing obedience and loyalty. Mayapán itself grew into a city of unprecedented size, heavily defended by a powerful encircling wall and holding an unusually large permanent population. Most of its important buildings were residential and administrative, and only a few religious buildings were constructed. All of them show a sharp decline in the level of artistic production and architectural imagination. In view of the enormous power concentrated at Mayapán this is an all the more significant illustration of the extraordinary cultural decline which had taken place.

Architects no longer used finely cut stones and bas-relief sculpture. Instead, the new structures were built of amazingly crude blocks of stone, which were covered with a thick veneer of stucco. The great colonnades of Chichén Itzá were repeated only in miniature. Instead of the traditionally splendidly carved stone columns poor, vaguely round pillars were erected, of rough-hewn stones filled out with rubble, the whole then being covered with heavy stucco to hide their jerry-built interior structure. The hard-to-build corbeled vault was largely abandoned, and so was the ceremonial ball game. There were six great ball courts at Chichén Itzá, but not one has been found at Mayapán. The same was true for road construction; the great stone roads of Classic times were still being used, like the Roman roads in medieval Europe, but no effort was made to extend them or even to keep them in proper repair.

The most significant illustration of the decline of Maya culture and the profound change of spirit is seen in the tombs of Mayapán. The offerings now consisted only of a few coarse, monochrome vessels and crudely made, showy incense burners. But the burials

of Mayapán chiefs were marked by unprecedented mass slaughter. In one case the remains of forty-one persons have been found interred with their chief, and one regal couple was buried with only a few potsherds of poor quality but with huge quantities of birds and animals, whose bones littered their grave when it was excavated. A profound change of values had taken place and the provision of masses of servants and foodstuff for the afterlife was considered more important than the offering of objects of beauty and refinement. Massive barbaric ostentation took the place of an earlier period's civilized appreciation of works of art and elegant objects of luxury.

Hunac Ceel's descendants, the Cocom dynasty, continued their oppressive rule without serious opposition until the appearance of a new, dynamic personality named Ah Xupan, the head of an aristocratic family which also claimed Toltec descent, the Tutul Xiu. They were lords of a feudal domain that included the ancient and impressive city of Uxmal, and were tributaries of Mayapán. Around the year 1450, Ah Xupan was able to engineer a revolt of discontented subject cities, and in the war that followed, Mayapán was sacked and the ruling Cocom was slain with all of his sons, except for one who was away in Honduras on a trading expedition. The great Cocom empire dissolved into a dozen or so city-states, each of which was ruled by another of the old feudal families who still claimed Toltec descent.

Now began a period of uninterrupted warfare between the rival cities and dynasties, and what remained of Maya civilization sank to even lower levels. Pyramids no longer were constructed, and stone temples gave way to large thatched huts of the same type as the very first temples of early Preclassic times. When the Spaniards began the conquest of Yucatán in 1541, enmity between Maya cities had reached a level where many gladly threw in their lot with the Spaniards in the hope of defeating their rivals. None realized that thereby they only speeded the day of enslavement of them all and the final destruction of their ancient civilization.

A similar historical development took place among the Maya of the Guatemala highlands. Here too, Toltec invaders at the close of the Classic Period introduced the militarism which brought to an end the ancient theocratic pattern. In time, one group achieved hegemony and dominated the highlands. These were the Quiché Indians, whose rulers claimed descent from Toltec invaders and whose home region was the shores of Lake Atitlán.

Together with the Cakchiquel Indians—their neighbors and frequent allies—the Quiché expanded to the south and conquered the coastal plains with their immense riches of cacao, whose beans were so precious and widely used that they fulfilled a role almost like that of currency at this time. But the incipient Quiché empire collapsed, and the peoples of the region were hopelessly locked in internecine warfare when the Spaniards arrived.

Both Yucatán and the Guatemala highlands quickly fell under Spanish domination, but in the dense lowland jungles of Petén and Chiapas, Maya independence lived on for another hundred and fifty years. Its last citadel was Tayasal, on a remote, easily defended small island in Lake Petén. Here descendants of the Itzá dynasty of Chichén Itzá had settled after they were driven from their ancient city, and under their rule Tayasal successfully resisted the Spaniards until 1697.

THE MIXTEC RENAISSANCE

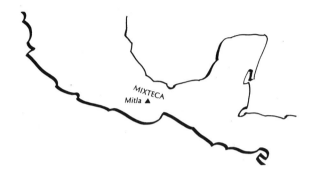

WHEN THE OLD CLASSIC CULTURES collapsed and their great temple-cities were abandoned and destroyed, the elaborate art they had produced died with them. It had already lost much of its vitality and creativeness before the final overthrow, and during the chaotic period that now followed, it entered its final phase of sad, sterile decadence. This was a period of great migrations, when energetic new peoples attained ascendancy and one of them developed an extraordinary new style that sparked a renaissance of the arts throughout Middle America. This creative new spirit was that of the powerful Mixtecs, and it was cradled in their highland valleys in Oaxaca and Puebla, lying just to the south and east of the Valley of Mexico. Because of its geographical center, some archaeologists have called the style Mixteca-Puebla, but the simpler term Mixtec has generally prevailed.

Although the style originated with the Mixtecs, its influence soon spread over an enormous area. Its precepts were followed from Sinaloa on the Pacific Coast, opposite the tip of Lower California, to Nicaragua and Costa Rica. It became the typical expression of the Historic Period, and it dominated the forms of the artistic renaissance that now developed. There is a striking parallel between the history of the Mixtec style and that of the European Renaissance, which also had its cradle in a small region—in central and northern Italy—and went on to set the standards for an entire continent.

The Mixtecs derived their name from their legendary home, the "land in the clouds," the mist-shrouded high sierras of Oaxaca. An early Preclassic culture has been excavated here at a site called Montenegro, dated at about 650 B.C. and showing strong Olmec influences. But it was not until the end of the Classic Period that the Mixtecs proper make their appearance in history, with the founding of the dynasty of the Lords of Tilantoga in A.D. 720. Before long they seem to have participated in—if not actually led—the conquest of the great city of Cholula in the Puebla highlands. Cholula became one of the important centers of Mixtec art and the home of the finest ceramic style in ancient Mexico.

The Mixtecs were the most intensive historians of Middle America; their splendid pictographic codices record without interruption the development of their people and rulers from the birth of Four Alligator, the first Lord of Tilantoga in the eighth century, until the last Mixtec cacique in 1580. The noted Mexican archaeologist and interpreter of the historical codices, Alfonso Caso, has suggested that Mixtec historiography arose out of the anguish and chaos that followed the collapse of Teotihuacán and the other Classic centers, and the need to record and interpret the great events that were so profoundly altering the world of that time.

In the Mixtec codices it is possible to read when a king was born, when he died, whom he married, what his victories and titles were, the places he conquered and by whom he was succeeded. The lives of many extraordinary personages are recorded in detail, such as Five Reed, the reformer of the calendar, and his still more famous son, the great conqueror Eight Deer Jaguarclaw. The latter's life is described in detail from his birth in 1011 and his investiture as chieftain in the imperial city of the Tula (in a ceremonial which

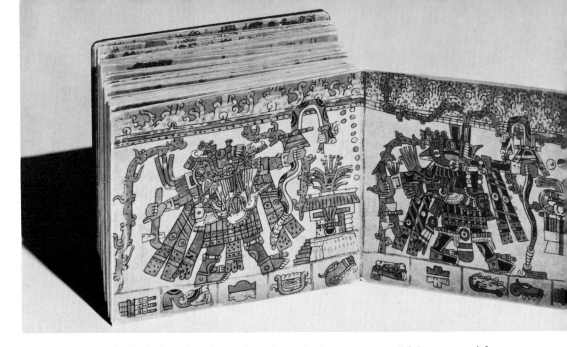

included the ritual perforation of the septum of his nose with an eagle talon or jaguar claw so that he could wear a ruler's distinguishing nose ornament) to his death in 1063. The codices tell of his wives, the Lady Six Monkeys and the Lady Thirteen Serpents, and they record his impressive list of victories and conquests and his voyages by land and water. In a final war in 1063 he was made prisoner and was sacrificed by his captors at the age of fifty-two years, the exact length of the ritual calendar's cycle of the planet Venus. His name is a good illustration of the ancient Indian custom of naming a child with the name of his birth date on the sacred calendar, such as Eight Deer. When a child reached the age of seven an individual name was then added to it, heroic or ferocious (such as Jaguarclaw) for men, flowery and pleasing for women. By the time of the Conquest the second name had become all-important and the calendrical birth-date name was hardly ever used.

Only a few examples of Mixtec historical literature have survived in a handful of codices: the Codex Nuttall; the Codex Vindobonensis, in the National Library, Vienna; the Codex Bodleian, in Oxford, England; and the Codex Colombino, one of the few ancient codices still preserved in Mexico. The other existing Mixtec codices deal chiefly with such subjects as the divinatory *tonalpohualli*, the

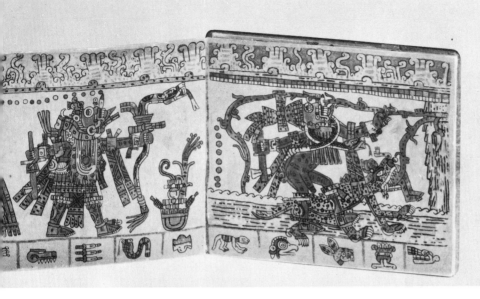

260-day ritual calendar, and the character and ruling aspects of the gods in the Mixtec pantheon. Among the most important and beautiful of these are the Codex Borgia and the Codex Vaticanus, both in Rome; and the Codex Laud and Codex Fejervary-Mayer, in England.

All of these books consist of long strips of leather, cotton cloth or bark paper, folded in screen fashion and sometimes placed between wooden covers. The background of each page was covered with gesso, and the scenes and ideographs were then painted in with flat colors outlined with a fine black or red line. The repertory of colors included a gold ocher, burnt sienna, carmine red, turquoise blue, olive green, gray, and black. The most elaborate representations are found in the miniature murals of the divinatory Mixtec codices with their complete cosmographic representations. They show the heavens with all their aspects and divinities, the interior of the earth, and the gods who inhabit these divine worlds and rule the fates of men. In general the Mixtec codices rely less than those of the Maya on glyph writing. They express the most complicated ideas through pictographic representations, which give full scope to the Mixtec talent for painting.

By the time of the Spanish Conquest, the Mixtecs and their Aztec pupils had developed a system of pictographs that was well on its

way to being turned into a fully phonetic script. During the transitional stage in which it was arrested by the Conquest, the rebus system was already in general use for geographical place names, which provide a good illustration of its method. For example, the name Quauhunahuac (today Cuernavaca) means "at the edge of the forest"; in the codices this was represented by a tree (*quau'-hitl*) and a mouth (*na'huatl*). Mixtlan, "the cloud land," was represented by a cloud (*mix'tli*) and a tooth (*tlan'tli*). Tochpan, (today Tuxpan), "the place of the rabbits," was indicated by a rabbit (*toch'tli*) and a flag (*pan'tli*).

The elaborate pictorial style developed in the codices was adapted to the extraordinarily fine ceramics of the Mixtecs. The ceramic industry seems to have been centered in Cholula, but much of its ware was exported and copied in other places. This pottery is distinguished most of all by its rich, dense polychrome, which combines such architectural elements as the stepped meander—probably representing an abstraction of a bird or serpent

head—with the most elaborate representations of divinities and
their attributes. Other vessels of a more domestic nature are en-
riched with enchanting stylizations of birds and butterflies, as well
as finely executed geometric motifs. One Mixtec vase gives clear
evidence of substantial influence from South America, in a design
copied exactly from a typical textile of the central coast of Peru.

A favorite form of the Mixtec potters was a spherical bowl
topped by a high cylindrical neck, the whole resting on three
flaring feet, sometimes in the form of serpents. Other typical shapes
include shallow drinking cups resting on flaring pedestals, and
high, straight-sided cylindrical cups also resting on a central pedes-
tal. The glowing, glossy surface of these vessels looks deceptively
like a glaze, but it is actually the result of careful, painstaking
burnishing with an agate or bone tool. Comparatively few clay
figurines were made by the Mixtecs, but at Teotilan del Camino,

in Puebla, a distinctive representation of deities was made whose form was based on hollow cylinders to which the image of a seated figure was adapted. Although polychromed, these figures were not burnished, and generally much of their paint has faded or flaked off. The gods represented are often shown wearing a beard, one of the attributes of Quetzalcóatl, even though the figures are thought to represent Macuilxochitl, the god of music, song, dance, poetry and the pleasures of the flesh. This is not an unusual occurrence, for especially in later Historic times many new and sometimes local representations of the gods appeared with various attributes borrowed from other, older gods. This interchangeability of characteristics plus the dual nature of the gods, their good and evil aspects which are expressed in their attributes and positions in the codices, make the ever-growing pantheon of the Historic Period exceedingly complicated and confusing.

Frequently found in Oaxaca are small, amulet-size stone figurines of gods or ancestors which locally are quite appropriately called *penates* (the Latin term for household gods). They represent squatting or standing men, their features incised with straight-line and circular or semicircular, drilled cuts typical of this period's mass-production techniques. Some are carved in a very summary fashion indeed, while others show fine detailing. Each has a small drilled perforation in back through which a string could be passed. The finest of them are carved out of jade or onyx, while others are cut out of more common stones. They bear a striking resemblance to the small *Tiki* ancestor figurines of the Marquesas Islands. This was pointed out by the late Miguel Covarrubias, who had intensively explored this and the many other odd similarities between objects found in Middle America and those found in various islands of the Pacific Ocean or in the lands bordering its farther shore.

The Mixtecs left little major stone sculpture, but they were masters in the art of carving hard, beautiful stones, and they took a special delight in the translucent qualities of tecali, the alabaster-like Mexican onyx. They carved superb bowls and vases out of this stone, generally following the refined forms of their ceramics. The most beautiful of them are decorated with splendidly sculptured effigies of monkeys, turkeys and rabbits, whose forms are adapted to the pear-shaped vessel. The animal's limbs and features stand out in bas-relief, while the head is usually carved in full three-dimensional form with considerable sculptural power. The monkey vessels show the long, sweeping tail swinging around the vessel like a tumpline, so that the animal appears to be carrying it as a load. The hands of the monkey are sometimes shown grasping his tail in realistic playfulness.

The essentially decorative, pictographic spirit of Mixtec art is most clearly evident in their fine carving in wood and bone. Magnificently detailed representations of the most elaborate mythological scenes have been found carved on jaguar-bone spatulas, and the carvings on the few surviving wooden drums are like pages out of the codices. The Mixtecs also developed the art of making mosaics with inlays of shell and precious turquoise. Mounted on wood,

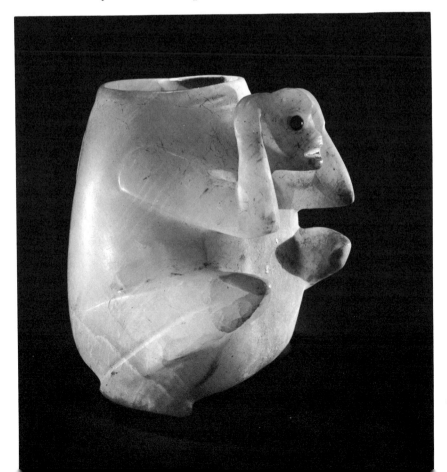

these mosaics served to decorate ceremonial shields and helmets, dance masks, scepters and the handles of sacrificial knives. Because of their perishable nature, only a very few have survived, chiefly in European museums. These reached Europe in the sixteenth century as trophies and souvenirs, thereby escaping the destructive censorship of the Spanish missionaries.

Early in the Historic Period the Mixtecs learned the art of finding and casting gold from the gold workers of Panama and Costa Rica. They took over all of the known techniques but brought them to a new pitch of refinement and delicacy. Cast wirelike filigree coils were a specially favorite device of Mixtec goldsmiths, who used it widely as an ideal device with which to express their taste for refined if somewhat crowded pictorial detail. Using gold, copper and occasionally silver, they made an enormous variety of objects and invented many unprecedented new forms. There are crowns and bracelets, disks and ornaments to be sewn on clothing that are hammered out of sheet gold and decorated with *repoussé* designs. There are myriads of small cast bells, in which they must have taken a special delight, judging by the quantities in which they are found. Excavations have brought to light a complete catalogue of jewelry, including rings, nail protectors, ear ornaments, necklaces, pendants, small masks and resplendent labrets, or lip plugs, which were worn through a perforation in the lower lip. The custom of wearing labrets was new with the Historic Period. It soon became a widely followed fashion among great personages and led to the creation of some of the finest and sculpturally most accomplished examples of Mixtec jewelry, usually in the form of eagle heads or great coiled serpents. Pendants were hung from these labrets, creating a splendid shimmering effect each time their wearer spoke or moved.

Although the Mixtecs began their metallurgy with borrowed techniques, the spirit and refinement of their jewelry was entirely their own, and they developed the art of the goldsmith to a level of perfection never attained before. The great treasure of gold and silver that Cortes saw at the court of the Aztec emperor Moctezuma

was probably entirely of Mixtec workmanship or Mixtec style. When the first presents that Moctezuma had offered to Cortes reached the court of Charles V in Brussels, they were seen there by Albrecht Dürer. On August 27, 1520 (a full year still before the fall of the Aztec capital of Tenochtitlán), the great artist wrote in his diary:

Also did I see the things which one brought to the King out of the new Golden Land: a whole golden sun, a full yard wide, similarly a whole silver moon, also equally big . . . all sorts of marvelous objects for human use which are much

more beautiful to behold than things spoken of in fairy tales. These things were all so precious that one has appraised them worth a hundred thousand guilders. And in all the days of my life I have seen nothing which so rejoiced my heart as these things. For I saw among them wondrous artful things and I marveled over the subtle genius of these men in strange countries. And I know not how to relate all of what I saw there before me.

The sober court historian Peter Martyr wrote about the same treasure in 1521 in Basel: "I do not marvel at gold and precious stones, but am in a manner astonished to see workmanship excel the substance."

The introduction of metallurgy into Mexico also saw the development of curious T-shaped copper blades. These seem to have been manufactured in enormous quantities and to have served along with such substances as cacao beans to fill the function of currency in the increasingly active trade that developed between the different regions of Middle America.

Another material that was first worked by the Mixtecs is rock crystal, a substance which looks like perpetual ice. It is extremely hard and difficult to work, but mechanically perfect cups, earplugs and small labrets in the shape of a top hat were often carved out of it. Mixtec lapidaries also made small animal figurines out of rock crystal, but it is questionable whether the famous human skulls are of pre-Conquest workmanship. It appears more likely that they are the product of early Spanish times, although made in the old Mixtec tradition and probably carved by the same artisans or their immediate descendants.

The one precious material which Mixtec craftsmen used with less skill than their predecessors was jade. Miguel Covarrubias has suggested that jade had become scarce by this time, especially the emerald-green jade so beloved by the Classic Maya. The few objects made of jade of this color during the Historic Period seem to use broken pieces of earlier cultures, while white jade mottled with

green, and green jade mottled with brown, now began to make their appearance. Mixtec jade carving is generally rather mechanical, usually relying on simple geometric lines and circular grooves made by tubular drills.

The most breathtaking array of Mixtec treasure came to light in 1931, when Alfonso Caso excavated the famous Tomb 7 on Monte Albán. This grand temple-city of the Zapotecs was taken over by the Mixtecs during the Historic Period and was used as a necropolis for the interment of important personages. The high dignitary who was buried in Tomb 7 was accompanied by an offering of every precious material known to his time—more than five hundred objects of jade and turquoise, shell, onyx, rock crystal and gold. The riches and perfection of his gifts are unique and form a glowing testimony to the extraordinary refinement reached by this great culture. At the same time, the tomb also offers evidence of the continuation into Historic times of ancient forms, such as the impressive ceremonial cup of *tecali*, a footed version of the old Preclassic oval bowl whose indented sides give it a figure-eight appearance. The most famous of Mixtec gold objects is the great gold pendant effigy of the head of a high priest wearing a great headdress made of filigree gold, which is now in the museum of Oaxaca along with the other contents of Tomb 7. It is interesting to note how, for glyphic calendric notations, this figure makes use of two large, rectangular, flat areas at the bottom of the pendant, whose form is obviously derived from Veragua jumping-frog prototypes.

Not far from Monte Albán rise the ruins of the temples and palaces of Mitla, one of the few known important Mixtec architectural monuments. The center was dedicated to the worship of Quetzalcóatl and was the residence of high priests at the time of the Conquest. Its extraordinary buildings have long been famous for their long horizontal lines, the perfection of their noble proportions and the rich mosaic effect of the walls. These represent countless variations of the favorite Mixtec motif of stepped Greek key and spirals called *xicalcoliukqui*, and are probably based on a

stylization of a bird or serpent head. They meander in endless procession over the inner and outer walls of the buildings at Mitla. At first glance, they would seem to be made up of mosaics of small inlaid stones, which is the way they were described by early visitors. Actually, the wall decorations are composed of quantities of small stone plaques on which the stepped-key designs were carefully chiseled out in bas-relief and which were then fitted together with the infinitely painstaking care that is a typical manifestation of the perfectionist spirit of Mixtec art.

In everything they did, Mixtec artists and craftsmen were enormously admired in their own day. Their accomplishments and style were followed and copied all over Middle America. The clearest evidence of the esteem in which they were held was seen at the court of the later Aztec emperors, where most of the splendid luxury objects that so dazzled Cortes and his followers were of Mixtec craftsmanship or style.

THE INVADERS

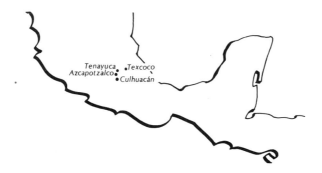

THE HORDES OF CHICHIMEC NOMADS who invaded the Valley of
Mexico under their dread chief Xólotl and destroyed Tula in 1224
were following the historical pattern of the preceding phase. Like
hungry wild animals around a camp site, they had long circled
around the borders of the fertile valley and its rich and powerful
cities. Then they attacked, conquered, and destroyed with fire and
sword, but before long they had settled down and adopted the ways
of the old population; and in time they forgot the barbarian customs of their nomadic days.

The codices depict Xólotl's followers dressed in rude deerskins,
primitives who lived in caves and hunted wild animals. Their
name, Chichimec, means "of dog lineage," signifying their tribal
totem animal. Within a very short time as history goes, the name
Chichimec became the proud title of a highly civilized ruling aristocracy and thus, like the term Toltec, ran the full gamut of con-
notation, from that of uncouth barbarian to that of admired progenitor of noble traditions.

After destroying Tula, Xólotl founded his capital at Tenayuca, while the chieftains of two important tribal groups who had followed him into the valley settled at Azcapotzalco and Xaltocán. To solidify their alliance Xólotl gave one of his daughters in marriage to each of these chieftains. The three cities thus formed the first of the famous triple alliances that were to dominate the Valley of Mexico during much of the next period. The enemy of the alliance, and the most important power against whom the alliance was formed, was the city of Culhuacán, the last refuge of the once dominant Toltecs.

The wars that followed saw the first use of a dreaded new weapon: the bow and arrow. It was the weapon of the barbarian hunters, and it gave them an insuperable advantage over an enemy who used only the atlatl and spearthrower. Another of the few innovations contributed by the Chichimecs was the architectural concept introduced in the pyramid they erected in Tenayuca. In what was perhaps a barbarian spirit of economy, they topped their pyramid with two sanctuaries, reached by two parallel ceremonial stairways. One of the chambers was dedicated to the tribal war god Tezcatlipoca, the limping god, whose right foot was replaced by a "smoking mirror"; the other was dedicated to Tlaloc, the ancient rain god of the old agricultural population. This pattern was later copied—but on a much grander scale—by the Aztecs when they built the great pyramid in their capital Tenochtitlán. The Aztec pyramid was destroyed by the Spaniards, but the pyramid of Tenayuca remained standing, and it has been extensively explored by archaeologists, who have discovered among other things that the compiled structure represented a final superimposition of pyramid on pyramid, the structures here reaching a total of five.

Xólotl did not have the good fortune to beget a son as illustrious as Quetzalcóatl, but he did become the progenitor of a royal lineage whose descendants occupied virtually all the thrones of Mexico until the Spanish Conquest. Xólotl's children and grandchildren ruled not only the Chichimec cities but through intermarriage his line was mixed with that of all the other ruling houses.

Under Xólotl's son and successor, Nopaltzin, the long struggle with Culhuacán was finally brought to a successful conclusion, and the Chichimecs achieved undisputed hegemony in the Valley of Mexico. Culhuacán remained independent under its ancient Toltec dynasty, but it was no longer powerful enough to be a threat. During the stable period which now followed, there was a new birth of civilization, a new beginning for the arts that had so long lain neglected during the years of invasion and war. The early Spanish chronicles report that during the reign of Xólotl's grandson Tlotzin a group called *regresados* ("returned ones") arrived in the Valley of Mexico and brought with them new crafts and techniques. Ignacio Bernal has suggested that they were the descendants of an elite of artisans who had fled from their destroyed cities during the Chichimec invasions and migrated to the valleys of the Mixtecs to the south and east. Returning now to their old homes, they brought with them the brilliant new Mixtec style, the exciting discovery of metalworking, new ceramic techniques, the forgotten arts of glyph writing and the recording of history in books—all of which were flourishing at this time in the Mixtec valleys of Puebla and Oaxaca. The chronicles record that the *regresados* were the founders of the city of Texcoco in 1327 and here taught these new arts to their Chichimec neighbors.

A deep split was created in the ranks of Chichimec leaders by these new developments. Many were deeply conservative and felt strongly that their tribe must not lose its sturdy old nomadic traditions. They feared the new culture and its softening effects; they saw it as undermining the strong, militant fiber of their tribes. There was a bitter struggle, but progress won and for once the partisans of culture emerged triumphant. A new dynasty was established in Texcoco by Xólotl's highly civilized great-grandson Quinatzin, who ruled until 1357 bearing the proud title of Grand Chichimec, a title which now stood for aristocratic refinement and noble rule. Under his enlightened leadership, and that of his descendants, Texcoco became the focus of all intellectual life of the valley, the possessor of the largest library of its time, and the center of Indian civilization.

During this period, the city of Azcapotzalco was rising to a position of power and influence in the Valley of Mexico. It had been founded by the Tepanecs from the neighboring Valley of Toluca in the thirteenth century. From that time it had grown and prospered. In 1363 an ambitious new ruler ascended its throne, the remarkable Tezozómoc. He was a man of brilliant intelligence and equal perfidy, a greedy, scheming, patient prince blessed with an exceptionally long life, which gave him some sixty-three years of rule and enabled him to see his grandiose power politics crowned with unprecedented success. As Ignacio Bernal has remarked, Tezozómoc was an even more perfect example of the application of Machiavelli's cynical precepts in *The Prince* than Cesare Borgia himself. His goal was the domination of all of Xólotl's heritage, and to achieve this he used war as a systematic weapon of expansion in combination with alliances, calculated treason, and carefully planned dynastic intermarriages, which in time settled his sons and grandsons on the thrones of most of the feudal domains of the Valley of Mexico.

Tezozómoc achieved the unification of most of the Valley of Mexico and became its virtually undisputed overlord. The larger of the city-states stood in terror of him, paid tribute and acknowledged his overlordship; the smaller domains, which had become so many tiny feudal holdings since the collapse of the Toltec empire, were now absorbed one after another into Tezozómoc's empire. This helped to prepare the way for the still greater and much more rigid unification that was to be imposed a generation or two later by the Aztecs, who at this time were only a small tribe of mercenaries in Tezozómoc's service.

The chronicles and codices tell the dramatic story of the bitter struggle between Tezozómoc and the ruler of Texcoco, who, as the direct descendant of Xólotl, claimed sovereignty over all the other Chichimec ruling families. Constant, ruinous warfare was waged, interrupted by only short-lived armistices and usually false promises of peace. Always plotting and intriguing, Tezozómoc kept nibbling away at Texcoco's established power. A crisis was reached in 1409, when Ixtlilxóchitl ascended the throne of Texcoco. To the solemn ceremony of his installation as Grand Chichimec he convoked a gathering of the heads of all the Chichimec clans. But Tezozómoc now claimed the title for himself, as a descendant of Xólotl in his own right and with a great force of arms to back him. As a result, only two chieftains attended the installation; the others pleaded various urgent excuses, but in fact they were intimidated by Tezozómoc's power.

Ixtlilxóchitl sought to reach a peaceful compromise by marrying one of Tezozómoc's daughters. This proved to be a futile gesture; the power-hungry tyrant's hostility continued unabated. Ixtlilxóchitl then formed an alliance with all the city-states which seemed threatened by Tezozómoc's ambitions. War was declared with all its time-honored formalities, and a great battle ensued in which Tezozómoc's forces were decisively beaten. The allies celebrated their victory and congratulated themselves on having once and for all beaten down the power that had disturbed the peace of the valley for decades. To Tezozómoc, however, the lost battle was only a temporary setback. With skillful diplomacy and enticing promises of spoils and territories, he managed to woo away his archenemy's former allies. When enough had switched sides or pronounced their neutrality, Tezozómoc assembled his warriors in secret and descended suddenly on now defenseless Texcoco, whose armies had long since been demobilized in what was thought to be a long and victorious peace. The year was 1418, and Ixtlilxóchitl found himself ignominiously forced to flee for his life accompanied only by a last remnant of faithful retainers and his small son Netzahualcóyotl ("the hungry coyote"). The vengeful Tezozómoc sent search parties after the small band, which found refuge only in a dense forest in a deep ravine.

The chronicles relate how Ixtlilxóchitl passed the night sleeping under a great fallen tree with two captains and his son. At sunrise they were wakened by a soldier who reported that they had been discovered and that a large force of Tezozómoc's soldiers were approaching to hunt them down. Knowing that the end was near and that the enemy sought only his death, he called his son to his side and spoke to him:

> My much beloved son, arm of a lion, Netzahualcóyotl, whence shall I send you, where will I find a friend or vassal who will receive and shelter you? This will be the last day of my misfortunes and it is hard for me to leave this life; what I want to enjoin on you and commend to you is never to abandon your subjects and your vassals, nor to forget or leave in oblivion that you are Chichimec, to reclaim your realm which Tezozómoc so unjustly tyrannizes and to avenge the death of your afflicted father. Nor forget to exercise your weapons, bow and arrow. And now it only remains for you to hide in these bushes so that the so very ancient empire of your ancestors will not perish with you.

From his hiding place the young prince saw his father cut down by the enemy soldiers. After they retired he recovered the body and with the help of the last few remaining friends buried it in a cave according to the fashion of his distant nomadic ancestors. Now began a long period of flight and exile for Netzahualcóyotl. As the only legitimate heir to the throne of the Grand Chichimec, he remained a bone in the throat of Tezozómoc. Pursued by the tyrant's implacable jealousy, he was forced to flee from one refuge to another. The chronicles relate innumerable dramatic adventures and hairbreadth escapes of the prince, who was to become the most admired and illustrious figure of his century.

Eventually, in 1426, Netzahualcóyotl was able to assume the Texcocan throne, when the usurper—full of years and bloody successes—died. Tezozómoc's empire quickly collapsed into a multiplicity of independent feudal principalities, while Texcoco soon regained its ascendancy over them. Under Netzahualcóyotl's enlightened rule, Texcoco became the intellectual as well as the political center of the Valley of Mexico. The new ruler achieved unparalleled prestige through the laws which he promulgated and codified and which became models widely copied by other city-states. Though they appear to us as rigid, puritanical, and brutal in their punishments, their impartial administration and their generally sobering effect were enormously admired in their own time. Under Netzahualcóyotl's personal aegis a large group of poets gathered at his court. He himself wrote poetry that became famous in his own time, and some of it has survived to our day. Typical of his reflective spirit are these lines:

The fleeting vanities of the world are like the green willow
Which the sharp edge of the axe cuts down and the wind uproots.

This enlightened ruler was also much influenced by the old legends and doctrines of Quetzalcóatl, who was still considered the original founder of the priesthood and whose name was carried as title by each high priest. Based on Quetzalcóatl's ancient precepts, an advanced, highly civilized cult was established which worshiped a single supreme deity who ruled over all the gods, who was conceived of as a pure spirit without embodiment, to whom no statues could be erected, and who required no human sacrifices. But this philosophic, abstract religion was followed only by a small circle at court; it found few adherents among the superstitious masses.

After the death of Netzahualcóyotl, in 1472, his son Netzahual-pili ("the hungry prince") ascended the throne. During his rule the cultural flowering of Texcoco entered into a decadent phase, and the city's great political power, bit by imperceptible bit, shifted to its partner in the triple alliance that dominated the highlands after Tezozómoc's death—to the parvenu capital of the Aztecs, Tenochtitlán.

During this period of incessant warfare, the visual arts did poorly in the Valley of Mexico. Fairly simple pottery was made in a style known as Aztec II, orange ware with designs painted in simple black lines, often with flat, slablike feet, on the Mixtec model. This was the prevailing type of pottery in the highlands right on through the subsequent Aztec empire, although designs were refined and became more elaborate during the later centuries.

A very distinguished type of pottery was made by the historic Totonacs of the Gulf Coast, who had built an important center at Cempoala. Its style is usually called Isla de Sacrificios after the important site on an island in the Gulf of Mexico where it was first and most abundantly found. Made of the fine buff-colored clay, the elegant shapes of this Totonac pottery were painted with bold white, red and black designs of animals and men. Like the splendid ceramics of the Mixtecs, it was much appreciated in its own time and actively traded over a wide area.

THE AZTECS

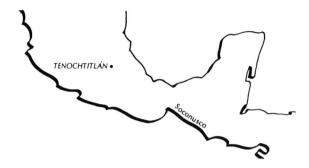

IN THE WAKE OF XÓLOTL'S CONQUERING HORDES, a small tribe of insignificant nomads followed the promising roads to riches to the Valley of Mexico and hovered about the new settlements of the powerful Chichimec tribes. This poor, ragged band came from a legendary home called Aztlán, "white place," on a lake in western Mexico. They were called Aztecs, the people from Aztlán. During their long migration they found, in a cave on the way, their tribal god Huitzilopochtli, "Left-handed Hummingbird." His first command to his people was that henceforth they call themselves México. But to history Huitzilopochtli's people remained known as the Aztecs.

They were little appreciated by their first neighbors. Their constant intrigues, raids and stealing of women caused a coalition of affronted city-states to send out a military expedition to dislodge the troublesome newcomers from their home on Chapultepec hill. They were summarily dealt with by superior forces and were enslaved as serfs of the Lord of Culhuacán. But fortune helped them when war broke out soon afterward between Culhuacán and the city of Xochimilco. The Aztecs rose in revolt against their masters and helped Xochimilco to win the war and themselves to win their freedom. Huitzilopochtli's priests now reported their god's new directions for finding a place of permanent settlement, a spot "where an eagle with a snake in its beak would land on a nopal cactus." The tribal sages promptly witnessed this event on a small, deserted, swampy island in the middle of Lake Texcoco, an occasion that is commemorated in the modern Mexican coat of arms and on every Mexican coin.

Actually, the selection of the isolated island was a brilliant political and strategic decision, the first demonstration of the Aztecs' special gift in this area. The easily defended and difficult-to-attack island was claimed by three contending city-states and thus was really subject to none. By occupying it the Aztec could lend their weight first to one, then to another of their neighbors and play them off against each other. At the same time the island enjoyed

superb communications by water with all of the important cities on the shores of connecting lakes that filled the center of the Valley of Mexico. In an age without draft animals, when human backs were the only carriers of goods over land, transportation over water, by canoe, was far more expeditious.

The Aztecs' tribal chieftain at this time was named Tenoch, and the small settlement of simple huts around the first unimpressive shrine to Huitzilopochtli was, therefore, called Tenochtitlán ("Tenoch's city"). To supplement the meager living which their poor island provided, the Aztecs continued to hire themselves out as mercenaries to Tezozómoc, the aggressive ruler of nearby Azcapotzalco. On his behalf they conquered Culhuacán, the last stronghold of the ancient Toltec dynasty.

By 1376 the Aztecs had prospered sufficiently to feel that they too needed a proper, aristocratic king of noble lineage like those of the other city-states in the valley. With great political shrewdness they did not offer their throne to the ruling family of Azcapotzalco as so many other small cities had done. Instead they chose as their sovereign a descendant of the last, now deposed ruler of Culhuacán's Toltec dynasty. Through their new ruler, Acamapichtli ("Hand of Cane"), and his descendants, the Aztecs obtained a claim to the rulership of the great Toltec empire and to all of its glory and prestige. It was a highly presumptuous claim for so insignificant a people to make; they were not even fully independent, but remained a feudal tributary and vassal of the feared and mighty Tezozómoc. But within a hundred years they were to make good this claim and rule over all of the former Toltec empire and much else besides.

With the election of their first king, then, the Aztecs took their first significant step toward empire. As part of their self-claimed heritage they also took over the ancient Toltec royal investiture ceremony which contained the fateful warning that would henceforth be recalled to each Aztec ruler as he ascended to the throne: "Remember that this is not your throne but that it is only lent to you and that one day it will be returned to Quetzalcóatl, to whom it truly belongs." Throughout their history one of the proudest titles claimed by the Aztec rulers was that of Lord of Culhuacán, for Culhuacán had been the first and the last capital of the old Toltec empire, and the title was an affirmation of the Aztecs' Toltec heritage. When the first Spaniards landed, in 1518 and 1519, in Tabasco and Veracruz and asked who was the ruler of the land, they were told Culhuatecuhtli, the Lord of Culhuacán. They did not get the name completely right but Hispanicized it and called the small island in the harbor of Veracruz on which they landed San Juan de Ulúa.

Under their first two kings the Aztecs continued their role of mercenaries for Tezozómoc and expanded his realm into the lovely Valley of Morelos. But during the reign of the third king, Chimal-popoca ("Smoking Shield"), the much feared old Tezozómoc died at last. No sooner was the tyrant buried than a civil war began between two contending heirs who contested the rule of his empire. Chimalpopoca made the unforgivable mistake of choosing sides too soon and found himself allied with the loser in the struggle. The victor hounded to death all those who had conspired against him; the unfortunate Chimalpopoca was first imprisoned and then hanged in 1427. The Aztec elders elected as their next ruler Izcóatl ("Obsidian Snake"), a brilliant son of their first king and a slave woman. His extraordinary personal qualities compensated for his incompletely royal descent.

Izcóatl was a political and military genius, who during his thirteen-year reign transformed the Aztecs from a small tribe of mercenaries into the founders of an empire. He understood that his predecessor's enemy had achieved only a Pyrrhic victory in his fight for the throne, and that Azcapotzalco had been seriously weakened. Izcóatl therefore initiated an alliance with Netzahual-cóyotl, the poet-king of Texcoco, and also with the ruler of the city of Tacuba. After a bitter and difficult struggle, the triple alliance conquered Azcapotzalco itself in 1428, although its ruler continued to make war from other, smaller fortified cities of his shrinking realm until his final defeat in 1433.

From this point on, the triple alliance dominated the highlands of Mexico. The partners made wars jointly, and they divided spoils and tribute according to a formula which accurately reflected the ratio of power within the alliance at this time: two fifths went to Tenochtitlán, two fifths to Texcoco and one fifth to Tacuba. During Netzahualcóyotl's lifetime, Texcoco was the dominant partner of the alliance; but slowly leadership shifted to Tenochtitlán until, by the time of the Spanish Conquest, Tenochtitlán had assumed virtual rulership over the other two cities.

After the successful conclusion of the war against Azcapotzalco, Izcóatl did not disband his warriors as was customary, but continued a campaign of conquest to establish Tenochtitlán's power over the cities which the Aztecs had previously conquered on behalf of Azcapotzalco. When Izcóatl died, in 1440, he was succeeded on the throne by another ruler with imperial instincts, the first Moctezuma ("Angry Lord"). During his reign a great drought struck the Valley of Mexico, and it was followed by a terrifying famine. The chronicles record that even the beasts of the mountains faced starvation and descended into the valley, where they attacked men. The roads were full of people dead of hunger being devoured by famished animals, while others in desperation sold themselves into slavery. To bring an end to the catastrophe, the Aztecs sent traders to the Totonacs on the Gulf Coast, whose rich tropical lands were unaffected by the drought, to buy and borrow corn and other foodstuffs. At home the Aztec priests instituted a system of mass human sacrifices on a scale never before known, to appease the angry gods.

The great drought lasted from 1450 to 1454. When it was over, Moctezuma determined to annex the fruitful regions of the Totonacs as the best guarantee against the occurrence of another famine. With cold-blooded calculation he returned the loan of corn by dispatching his troops to the coast and, in a series of ferocious, unexpected attacks, conquered most of the modern state of Veracruz.

Moctezuma perfected the Aztec military technique of blitzkrieg. The strategy called for sudden, unexpected attacks in which the well-organized professional soldiery of the Aztecs would overwhelm the generally poorly organized resistance of their victims with calculated violence and brutality. Once the battle was won and the enemy chieftain captured, the Aztecs proceeded to burn the conquered city's temple as a signal of victory. The soldiers stayed only long enough to divide the loot and the women, and the prisoners were sent to Tenochtitlán to be sacrificed to the greater glory of Huitzilopochtli. A heavy tribute was fixed, to be sent every six months to the cities of the triple alliance, and a local government was set up subject to the orders of Tenochtitlán. This done, the armies marched on to subjugate new territories or to quell with ruthless terror the occasional uprisings or rebellions that took place among their oppressed tributaries. In this manner the Aztecs conquered most of the Gulf Coast, the highland valleys of Puebla and Oaxaca, Guerrero, and Soconusco, the rich region on the Pacific Coast of the Isthmus of Tehuantepec.

Moctezuma was not only a military conqueror but also a great builder. Under his rule the best architects of the time, the builders of Chalco, were brought to Tenochtitlán to initiate the transformation of the capital from a small provincial town chiefly composed of simple thatched huts into a great metropolis of brilliantly painted stone temples and palaces. Moctezuma also possessed the great love of flowers which was such a typical trait of his people, and which has a curious parallel in the Japanese Samurai warriors' fondness for flowers. In a lovely valley near Cuernavaca, Moctezuma created a true botanical garden, with rare flowers brought from all the different parts of his realm. The garden was maintained by his successors but fell into neglect after the Spanish Conquest. There is still an orchard in the region which is pointed out to visitors as "the garden of Moctezuma."

At this time the religious system of the Aztecs was established. Various deities were taken over from subject peoples, and Huitzilopochtli was elevated from a purely tribal god into the category of a major creator deity. Along with his original manifestation as a tribal god with many of the attributes of the war god Tezcatlipoca, Huitzilopochtli was now the sun, the giver of light and warmth and all the things necessary to life itself, and the ruler of all the days. As the sun, Huitzilopochtli was believed to be engaged in an epic struggle each night with his enemies, the jaguars of darkness, who were represented by the moon and the stars. Thus the sacred duty fell to the Aztecs, Huitzilopochtli's people, to feed and sustain the sun with the nourishment it needed, the most precious of all foods, the very nectar of the gods: human blood. This horrifying cosmic image and the gory rites that were instituted in response to it were part of the strong motivation for the perpetual state of war in which the Aztecs lived, for only by war could sufficient captives be obtained to satisfy the bloodthirsty priests of Tenochtitlán. To feed the gods during the occasional periods of peace, a system of symbolic "flower wars" was arranged by the Aztecs and some of their neighbors. On an appointed day two opposing teams of warriors engaged in a great mock battle at a predetermined site with the object of catching the largest number of prisoners. Each side then would take its prisoners to its temples and offer them to its gods.

At the same time, the need for sacrificial prisoners was by no means the only reason for war. Since the days of Mixcóatl, war had been a more or less permanent feature of life, and the entire Historic Period was dominated by warriors, in contrast to the more peaceful, priest-dominated Classic Period. After the collapse of the Toltec empire, the perpetual feuds of the competing domains and the inroads of the Chichimec invaders only accentuated this state of affairs. The devastating contribution of the Aztecs was to exploit war as an instrument of policy and systematic conquest. War enabled them to build an enormous, unified empire and to impose an unprecedented degree of central control.

Another feature of Aztec society was the increasingly important role played by the traders and merchants. They organized large trading expeditions to regions as distant as Panama, and the intelligence they brought back was used to plan further conquests. Many trading posts were established and—as in the course of European colonization from the sixteenth to the nineteenth century—trade was usually followed by the flag.

In 1469 Moctezuma died and was succeeded by his son Axayá-catl ("Face of Water"), who continued the wars of conquest and the expansion of the empire. The formerly allied city of Tlatelolco was conquered, and Axayáctl killed its last king with his own hands after the storming of that poor city's chief pyramid. Further expansion took place into the Valley of Toluca to the west, but at its farther edge the Aztecs met the only enemy whom they could not conquer with sheer force of arms, the fierce Tarascans of Michoa-cán. At their hands the Aztecs suffered in 1480 their only serious defeat in battle. A kind of persistent "cold war" then ensued, each side building a long line of fortresses along the common frontier roughly overlapping the present-day border between the states of Michoacán and México, and running down from there through Guerrero to the Pacific Coast.

The Tarascans were a militant group who after the tenth century had expanded from their ancestral home on the shores of Lake Patzcuaro until they had conquered all of the present-day state of Michoacán. Excavations of their capital city of Tzintzuntzan have brought to light the remains of a considerable city with character-istic T-shaped, terraced temple bases called *yacatas* and much evi-dence of their extraordinary skill as potters and metalworkers. They mined copper and were able to cast superbly intricate ornaments as well as weapons, and it was in part due to the su-periority of their copper weapons that the Tarascans were able to resist so successfully the well-organized Aztec armies. Another art which the Tarascans developed with special skill was the carving of hard, brittle, smoky-black obsidian into earplugs and labrets so fine and thin that they are translucent. Characteristic too are rather crude volcanic-stone figures including frequent representa-tions of the old Toltec image of a reclining god holding a bowl, the "Chac-Mool."

In Tenochtitlán the reign of Axayácatl continued until 1481 and was marked by the beginning of the grand period of Aztec art. Con-

struction was begun on the huge temples and palaces that so dazzled the followers of Cortes. The awesome, monumental basalt sculptures of the terrifying gods of the Aztec pantheon also date from this period. Axayácatl was succeeded by Tizoc ("He Who Pierces Himself"—an allusion to ritual bloodletting), whose short and apparently unsuccessful reign was ended when he died of poison, probably intentionally administered. He was followed in 1486 by his brutal brother Ahuizotl ("Water Beast"), whose name is still invoked to frighten Indian children. The outrages that were committed during his reign were remembered with unforgiving bitterness by the Aztecs' subject peoples. This had the most profound and disastrous consequences for the Aztecs after Cortes's arrival in 1519.

During the first year of Ahuizotl's reign the great pyramid of Tenochtitlán was completed with its twin sanctuaries to Tlaloc and Huitzilopochtli. The inauguration festivities lasted four days and were accompanied by the slaughter of sacrificial victims in such staggering numbers that the event left an indelible mark in Indian memory. The emperor continued the traditional policy of military conquests and expanded the frontiers of the Aztec realm until they reached Guatemala, while the annual tribute lists grew ever larger. In 1502 there were unusually heavy rains and the water level of Lake Texcoco rose until one of the protective dikes suddenly gave way and Tenochtitlán was inundated. Trying to flee from his palace, Ahuizotl was struck by a falling beam and died.

Ahuizotl was the last of the great military chiefs of the Aztec state. The emperor who was elected to succeed him, the second Moctezuma, was a man of a profoundly different mold. He too had begun his career as a soldier and had proven his valor in battle. But he was a deeply religious man, completely involved in the priestly life to which he had turned in the observance of religious ceremonies and the interpretation of omens and augurs.

The people whom Moctezuma ruled differed as much from the simple mercenaries who had settled a small, swampy island under

the chieftain Tenoch as their splendid metropolis differed from the thatched huts of the first settlement. They were a refined, civilized people with a highly developed taste for music, dancing and poetry, flowers and decorations. Their architects built admirable temples and palaces, and their engineers constructed ingenious dams and aqueducts to carry fresh water to the island city from the mountains across the bay. They imported, through trade and tribute, the finest materials from distant regions and, along with them, the foreign artisans to work them into products of great luxury and beauty. Their nobles dressed themselves in regal mantles of cotton from the Gulf Coast and shimmering mosaics of rare quetzal feathers from the distant mountains of Chiapas and Guatemala. They graced their bodies with jewelry of finely cast gold and silver, carved jade and inlaid turquoise. Their food was served in bowls of elegantly painted ceramics and they drank chocolate from cups richly polychromed by the skilled Mixtec potters of Cholula.

The Aztecs drew to their island capital the best artists and craftsmen of all Mexico. A dynamic fusion took place, and many of the old arts that had ceased to be creative were imbued with a fresh spirit and vitality. Under Aztec aegis an imposing new style of sculpture was developed, tremendously energetic, often austere, of sweeping force and great dramatic impact, an art meant to inspire awe and impress a populace with the power of an empire and its gods. The favorite materials of these sculptors were basalt and other hard stones which could be precisely carved and could take such a high polish that they would shimmer darkly in sanctuaries or brilliantly reflect the rays of the sun. Their works were painted with a bright rainbow of colors that have been washed away but can be reconstructed from the small traces remaining in corners and crevasses.

The most dramatic monuments of Aztec art are the immense statues and altars which date from the time of the construction of the great temple, during the second half of the fifteenth century. A well-known example is the so-called Aztec calendar stone, made famous by hundreds of reproductions, which is really a votive stone that was made for the great temple. The complicated, elaborately detailed design represents the face of the sun in the center of the circular stone's thirteen-foot diameter, surrounded by the symbols of the four mythical prehistoric periods of Aztec cosmology, by the four directions of the compass and by the twenty day-signs of the Aztec month, and finally by two giant serpents which represent the sky that surrounds and supports the sun. Carved in the same precise bas-relief style is the Stone of Tizoc, a basalt cylinder on which this emperor is depicted wearing the attributes of a

god while holding by the hair—symbolic of taking captives—the lords of fifteen cities conquered by his people.

Still more monumental are the awe-inspiring, larger-than-life representations of the Aztec gods which struck such terror into the hearts of the first Spanish soldiers. A good example is the immense figure of the goddess Coatlicue, the mother of the gods. She is represented with such fearsome attributes as a necklace of sacrificed hands, hearts and skulls, and she wears a skirt of writhing snakes. Huge claws are shown growing on her feet, and she has not one but two heads, each like that of a twin-fanged serpent. Her mono-

lithic form is more than ten feet high and still, today, looms like a nightmarish apparition of death, terror and despotism.

At the same time, Aztec art had a naturalistic, anecdotal aspect that keeps breaking through again and again, producing the most beautiful examples of their sculpture. They observed closely the creatures they admired so much, eagles and frogs, dogs and coyotes, jaguars, grasshoppers, rabbits and even fleas. They represented them with a fidelity based on intimate understanding and with an extraordinary sculptural power not equaled since Olmec days. There are magnificent coiled snakes carved with such realism that they show the muscles rippling under the skin in the shining black basalt; and mythical animals like the famous feathered coyote, whose existence is made believable by the art of their creators.

Great love of life and delight with its gifts are reflected in a splendid pumpkin of green diorite and a black basalt nopal cactus. There are also extraordinarily sensitive portrayals of men and women; the noble portrait of the Eagle Warrior wearing the helmet of his order is a famous example. There are many infinitely appealing figures of the goddess of flowers and the goddess of water in the guise of kneeling young girls. They are shown wearing the modest *quexquemitl* cape, which is still seen today on Indian women, and beautifully detailed hair and headdresses made of paper fans that are reminiscent of the starched caps of Dutch or Breton peasant women.

One of the unique achievements of the Aztec stone carvers is the rock temple at Malinalco to the west of Mexico City, built between 1501 and 1515. This temple was dedicated to the military orders of the jaguar and the eagle and was carved out of the living rock, an immense artificial cave. The portal has been badly destroyed but appears to have represented the open jaws of the earth monster through which one entered into its realm, represented by the inner temple. This is a perfectly circular chamber surrounded by a stepped bench on which are raised in powerful, realistic relief the alternating forms of jaguar skins and eagles while in the center of

the floor another eagle rises. The entire temple represents a staggering technical achievement. All of its contents and sculptures were
carved out of the mountain's unforgiving rock. Even the smallest
mistake would have been fateful to its perfect symmetry.

Along with the formal monumental sculpture for their temples
and the more intimate masterpieces for the private enjoyment of
great nobles and priests, the Aztecs produced quantities of stone
and clay figures for worship in the temples and homes of the common people. The stone figures are usually carved in a massive,
geometric style reminiscent of Toltec tradition, often out of a
creamy-white stone whose surface was painted in bright, vivid
colors, or out of gray volcanic rock. Clay molds were used to manufacture rather stiffly stylized figurines of two highly popular deities, Xochiquetzal ("Flower Feather"), the goddess of love, flowers
and craftsmen, and Xochipilli ("Flower Prince"), her husband,
who ruled over the earthly pleasures of feasting and frivolity.

Typical Aztec domestic pottery continued the forms developed
in the Valley of Mexico during the preceding centuries, especially
the shallow bowl or plate on three angled slab feet, which was so
typical of the Historic Period. Many of these objects have a serrated
bottom, which was used as a grater for peppers. An interesting
feature of their decoration is that their designs become more realistic and less stylized with the passage of time, progressing from almost geometric abstractions in Period I to detailed representations
of birds and animals in Period IV, in the conventional classification
of Aztec pottery.

The finest luxury wares continued being imported from Mixtec
centers such as Cholula, and Mixtec style was evident in the designs of wooden drums, ceremonial atlatls and spear throwers, and
in the work of the goldsmiths. Among the most sumptuous manifestations of the Aztecs' growing taste for opulence were the un-
believably brilliant feather mantles, shields and headdresses of
their great personages. Unfortunately, only a very few have survived; pre-eminent among these are some of Moctezuma's original
gifts to Cortes which were preserved by the Hapsburgs. Among the

examples that still exist are a feather fan of the type that was carried on tall poles over great lords as an emblem of rank; a shield with a finely detailed mosaic of feathers highlighted with gold representing a plumed coyote, the glyphic emblem of the Emperor Ahuizotl; and a towering feather headdress with gold ornaments and a large bird's head of gold, which was stolen during the eighteenth century. Only six other examples of Aztec feather work remain; only one is in Mexico City, where it was returned from the Hapsburg collection during the 1860s as a good-will gesture by the ill-fated Emperor Maximilian.

The Aztec codices lacked the pictorial, iconographic perfection of the Mixtec books, even though the Aztecs had learned the art of bookmaking from the Mixtecs. Aztec codices have a much freer, more popular, reportorial style; in some ways they can be compared to our own comic strips. The Aztec images are more human; even the complicated attributes of the gods are never so overwhelming that the essential human features of each divinity are not clearly recognizable.

The most famous of the Aztec codices is the Codex Borbonicus in the Paris National Library. It consists of thirty-eight pages, each about fifteen inches square and folded like a screen, with a width of some forty-six feet when fully unfolded. The first twenty pages are devoted to the 260-day *tonalpohualli*, or ritual calendar, and each individual page is devoted to one thirteen-day week and shows the constellation of gods under which the time segment stands. The remaining eighteen pages contain a description of the ceremonies that mark the 365-day civil calendar, which was divided into eighteen 20-day months. The descriptive pictorial style of these books is one of the few arts which survived the Conquest for any length of time. It continued to be used in Spanish times in books which mix very successfully the style of the Aztecs and that of sixteenth-century Europe to describe for the benefit of the conquerors the history, customs and religion of the Indians. Among the most famous and enlightening of these is the Codex Florentino, compiled for Fray Bernardino de Sahagún by the pupils of his famous school in Tlatelolco.

The same pictorial style was also used for the tribute lists, which recorded in minute detail the kinds and quantities of goods that each subject city and region was compelled to send to Tenochtitlán at regular intervals. These amounted to such impressive totals as 140,000 bushels of corn, 105,000 bushels of beans, 105,000 bushels of seeds to be squeezed for oil, 6,000 loaves of salt, 36,000 bundles of tobacco, 1,260 man-sized loads of cacao beans, 1,600 man-sized loads of red pepper, 1,700 jars of honey, 4,800 bales of cotton, 32,880 bundles of quetzal and other feathers, 12,000 woven mats and the same number of stools, and a staggering 187,560 loads of white and colored blankets. There were quantities of firewood, planks, wooden beams for construction, reeds to be used as arrows, painted and lacquered gourds, 48,000 sheets of paper, 16,000 rubber balls, and innumerable quantities of incense and other materials for ritual temple uses. The distant province of Soconusco on the Pacific Coast at the Guatemalan border sent such specialties as forty jaguarskins, gold-encased rock crystal labrets, and whole blocks of precious raw rock crystal the size of adobe bricks.

Life was good in Anáhuac ("Land on the Water's Edge") for the lords of that world. Their splendid white city, crisscrossed by canals, provided them with all the luxuries of an empire and enabled them to enjoy, with all their senses, the good things of this life. Fifteen generations of successful, aristocratic ancestors separated them from the ragged nomads who had come to this valley in the wake of Xólotl, and they took for granted their aristocratic pleasures and privileges. They worshiped cruel gods as well as kindly ones. Their priests appeased Huitzilopochtli's constant need for bloody sacrifices with foreign victims brought by eager young warriors anxious to prove their manhood and valor; in return, apparently, the gods sustained the Aztecs in all their endeavors. Granaries and imported foodstuffs had abolished the fear of famine, and dikes controlled the angry flood of the waters. To be sure, there were occasional rumblings among distant tribes who rebelled at the tribute exacted from them, but the splendid Aztec armies soon quelled the troubles and the altars of the gods were replenished with fresh sacrifices.

In the meantime there was an empire to be administered and a graceful, civilized life to be enjoyed. There were solemn rites to be performed and honors to be vied for, markets to be visited, new poems to be heard and new foods from distant lands to be tasted, foaming cups of cocoa and even intoxicating pulque to revive a tired spirit in one's old age, when the prohibition against drunkenness no longer applied. Then, suddenly, on a cloudless April morning in 1519, the terrible news came by swift runners from the coast: Quetzalcóatl had returned!

Cortes had landed, with some five hundred followers, and they seemed to fulfill the dreaded ancient promise of Quetzalcóatl. The strangers had come across the water from the east, they followed a light-skinned, bearded leader, and they had come during the calendar's fateful period of Ce Acatl, ("One Reed"). That they also came with magic power was documented by the reports of their firearms, and the strange, fierce animals they rode—horses, which until then had been unknown in America.

Deep in his heart Moctezuma knew the end had come. First, however, he attempted to enlist the support of the other gods through prayers and propitiations, and to obtain their help in persuading Quetzalcóatl to desist from reclaiming his throne. Then he sent noble messengers to Cortes bearing the sacred insignia of Quetzalcóatl from the temple treasure chambers—the mask of gold, the feather headdress, the serpent mask—to convince him that his divinity was recognized and that there was no need for him to return in person. The royal presents did indeed convince Cortes—convinced him that he must conquer this rich and promising land. He promptly ordered the burning of his ships and with his small, adventurous band began the awe-inspiring foray across the mountains to Anáhuac and the fabled city of Tenochtitlán.

Moctezuma vacillated fatefully. When the Spaniards were at Cholula, he prepared a surprise attack, but the plan was betrayed. Cortes countered with a blood bath, partly for revenge and partly as a terrible warning of things to come. Then Moctezuma received Cortes and his followers; he not only permitted them to enter the city unchallenged but also lodged them in one of his own palaces. Appeasement followed appeasement, and Moctezuma was made to suffer the most unbearable humiliations—Cortes made him a prisoner in his own palace and even had him chained. This was the emperor whom none could approach except barefoot and with downcast eyes. Cortes forced him to watch passively the burning alive of the brave captain whom Moctezuma had ordered to attack the Spanish base on the coast. Still Moctezuma continued to do the Spaniards' bidding, while his nobles and priests became increasingly restless and urged him to renounce these unwanted guests who seemed to be making themselves lords of the country.

But Moctezuma was paralyzed by a profound inner sense of helplessness and a conviction of defeat. He complied with all of Cortes's wishes, though with a heavy heart, and at last said to him, "What more does Malinche [the Indian name for Cortes] want from me? I neither wish to live nor to listen to him, to such a pass has my fate brought me because of him." Notwithstanding this, he climbed once more to the ramparts of the palace in which he was held prisoner and which in turn was beleaguered by his own people. There he addressed them and urged them to desist from rioting against the Spaniards. While he spoke, some stones were thrown from below; whether they were meant for his Spanish guards or for him is uncertain. Moctezuma was hit, and although his wounds at first appeared to be slight, he died of them soon afterward, and perhaps also of a sick and broken heart.

A new emperor succeeded to power when the news became known, the fierce and brave warrior Cuauhtémoc, who saw the Spaniards not as gods but only as enemies to be killed or driven out. During the famous *Noche Triste* the Spaniards were attacked and forced to flee for their lives. Many were killed on the causeways leading from Tenochtitlán to the mainland or captured and sacrificed on Aztec altars.

Cortes and his surviving soldiers found refuge with the Tlaxcalans, the hereditary enemies of the Aztecs, and the Spaniards' first allies. Here they recuperated and reorganized themselves, and now war began in earnest. Cortes had found the fatal weak spot of the Aztec empire in the discontent of the subject peoples. With brilliant diplomacy he exploited this ferment of rebellion to make allies out of half the cities of the valley. Finally, in May 1521, Cortes felt strong enough to undertake an all-out attack on Tenochtitlán with the help of an immense number of Indian allies. Spanish records have always obscured the number of Indians who fought with them, but Cortes divided his army into three parts and the group he led alone counted 150,000 Indian warriors.

The siege of Tenochtitlán lasted eighty-five days and was brought to an end only by starvation and the systematic destruction of the city, house by house, which Cortes had ordered, to the delight of his Indian allies. For them the city had long been the symbol of their oppression; now they gladly joined in tearing it down. The rubble was dumped into the city's many canals. Ever since, Mexico City has been a veritable mine of Aztec sculpture; many fine old pieces come to light every time an excavation is made—usually for a new office building—in the downtown area.

What little was left of Tenochtitlán fell on August 13, 1521, when the Spaniards took the northeast corner of the city, the quarter where Cuauhtémoc and his few surviving followers had put up a last heroic resistance. Thus disappeared a city which had dazzled even the Spaniards. The most literate of them, Bernal Diaz del Castillo, had written that "we were amazed and said that it was like the enchantments they tell us of in the story of Amadis, on account of the great towers and pyramids and buildings rising from the water, and all built of masonry."

With the fall of Tenochtitlán the final curtain began to ring down on the great Indian civilization of Middle America. Spanish conquistadors, the gold and silver mines and sugar plantations they started, the brutal slavery which ensued, the missionaries and the new faith they brought, and the smallpox, colds and other European diseases to which the Indians had no resistance—all contributed to the total destruction of this culture. The glorious achievements were destroyed by greed and superstition and finally covered by dust and neglect. Only in recent times have they begun to be understood and appreciated again, as stone by broken stone and object by splendid object they are uncovered by the voracious power shovels of builders and the patient spades of archaeologists.

NOTES ON THE ILLUSTRATIONS

FRONTISPIECE: Life-size Maya stucco head. This sensitive portrayal of a young dignitary was found in tomb discovered inside Temple of Inscriptions at Palenque. (See photographs on pp. 127 and 135.)

PAGE 6: Seated Mezcala figurine; green diorite; 4¼″ high.

PAGE 20: Tlatilco vase of burnished black pottery with carved decorative neck band; 9″ high. AMNH.

PAGE 21: *Top:* Figurine from Santa Cruz, Morelos; 3″ high. *Bottom:* "Pretty Lady" (type D-1) figurine from Tlatilco; 3″ high.

PAGE 22: Female figurine from Santa Cruz, Morelos; 6″ high. Note *pastillaje* technique used on eyes and headdress (see also figurines on p. 21).

PAGE 23: Seated female figurine from Santa Cruz, Morelos; 7″ high. Collection Michel Warren.

PAGE 24: *Top:* Cylindrical seal from Tlatilco; 3″ high. Collection Jay C. Leff. *Bottom:* Seal representing a bird; 2″ wide. AMNH.

PAGE 25: Twin female figurines; 11½″ high. Collection Mrs. Bernard Gimbel.

PAGE 26: Fish effigy plate, excavated in Oaxaca; 12″ long. Collection Jay C. Leff.

PAGE 27: *Top:* Effigy vessel of a pullet, found at Tlatilco; 8″ high. Collection Baron Philippe de Rothschild. *Center:* Frog effigy vessel with incised design, found at Tlatilco; 6″ long. MAI—HF. *Bottom:* Stirrup-spout vessel from Tlatilco; 7″ high.

PAGE 29: *Top:* Chupícuaro figurine; 2½″ high. *Bottom:* Mammalian bowl from Chupícuaro; 6″ diameter. Collection Myriam Prévot.

PAGE 30: Chupícuaro hollow figurine with polychrome decorations; 9″ high.

PAGE 31: "Gingerbread" figurine; 13½″ high.

PAGE 32: Jalisco figure of woman holding a bowl; gray pottery with slip of fine white clay; 18½″ high.

PAGE 33: Colima figure of warrior; 24″ high. Collection Dr. Norman Simon.

PAGE 34: Colima group figurine—festive

Indians around tree with many birds perched on branches; 11″ high. AMNH.

PAGE 35: *Left:* Colima warrior with sling-shot, wearing helmet and large back ornament of bird feathers; 3″ high. Note whistle imbedded in head. On his right, Colima figurine of a stag, also with imbedded whistle; 2½″ high. *Right:* Colima figurine of woman grinding corn on a *metate;* 2½″ high. MAI—HF.

PAGE 36: *Top:* Colima figurine of transitional period when new, hollow figurines were being made, but with the stylization of the old, flat, solid figurines; 16″ high. *Bottom:* Colima sleeping dog; 9½″ wide. AMNH.

PAGE 38: *Top:* Colima cargo carrier; 10″ high. Note tumpline which passes around the carrier's head, back to the bottom of the large vessel on his back. This traditional Indian method of carrying heavy weights is still followed in many parts of Mexico and Guatemala. *Bottom:* Colima pumpkin bowl supported by three parrots; 9″ high, 13″ diameter.

PAGE 39: Nayarit figurine of woman wearing an apron; 15″ high. Note negative painting designs on her breast and stomach.

PAGE 40: Woman kneeling in childbirth position; Nayarit; 15″ high.

PAGE 41: *Top:* Nayarit figurine of sick man; 8″ high. Note protruding ribs, stylized tears flowing from the eye. *Bottom:* Nayarit figurine of sick woman; 9″ high.

PAGE 43: Head (8″ high) of a very large (28½″ high) Nayarit figure. Note traces of negative paint decorations on face and neck, and typical black-spotted patina. AMNH.

PAGES 44-45: Colima and Nayarit figurines of dancers, musicians, and a woman carrying a large bowl, in front of a Colima house model. Figurines are from 2″ to 3½″ high.

PAGE 46: Nayarit house model; 16″ high. AMNH.

PAGE 47: Nayarit village scene. Diameter of platform 8¾″. AMNH.

PAGE 49: Guerrero female figurine of coarse reddish pottery with white lime surface; 9″ high. Note typical incision running from collarbone to navel. Collection S. Dubiner.

PAGE 51: Jade figurine; 5″ high.

PAGE 52: Monumental Olmec head, known as Monument 1, of San Lorenzo, Veracruz; basalt; 9′ 4″ high, 6′ 6″ diameter.

PAGE 54: Olmec jade figurine from La Venta; 3½″ high.

PAGE 55: Famous cache of La Venta—sixteen jade and serpentine figurines and six jade celts; known as Offering No. 4. Figurines are from 6½″ to 7½″ high. Compare similar figurine shown on p. 54. Photograph by Philip Drucker, courtesy *National Geographic* Magazine, © National Geographic Society.

PAGE 56: Figurine (known as the "Tuxtla Statuette") of man in disguise of duck-billed bird; jade; 6″ high. Found at San Andres Tuxtla, Veracruz. U.S. National Museum, Washington.

PAGE 57: *Top:* Olmec jade effigy ax known as the "Kunz ax"; 11″ high. Note the dramatic fusion of human and feline features in the face. AMNH. *Bottom:* Olmec jade figurine of man-jaguar; 4″ high. Found at Necaxa, Puebla. AMNH.

PAGE 58: Olmec-type monument of incised gray stone; 10″ high. AMNH.

PAGE 61: Olmec jade mask; 5″ high. Collection Jay C. Leff.

PAGE 63: Problematic Olmec object of gray stone; 6″ high. It appears likely that the use of the so-called "miniature yokes" of this type is closely associated with the ceremonial ball game, in which they may have been worn or carried, in a manner not yet fully understood. AMNH.

PAGE 64: Olmec wooden mask with jade encrustations; 7½″ high. Found in cave in State of Guerrero. AMNH.

PAGE 65: Two of *Danzante* figurines of Monte Albán.

PAGE 66: Pyramid E-VII Sub at Uaxactún. Note stele on left, in front of main stairway.

PAGE 68: *Top and Bottom:* This blue-green jade pendant is the lower torso of Olmec figurine reworked in later times with Mixtec techniques; 2⅝″ high. In top picture, Mixtec face can be seen, its features marked with typical Mixtec hollow-core drills. In bottom picture, ornament is reversed, clearly showing original Olmec torso.

PAGE 72: Mezcala stone mask; 8″ high. Note the imitation of typical pottery techniques in the making of the eyes and mouth. Collection Mr. and Mrs. Werner Abegg.

PAGE 75: *Top:* Mezcala temple model of polished dark-green diorite; 3¼″ high. *Bottom:* Mezcala votive fish; 2¼″ long. Collection Alan Wardwell.

PAGE 76: Mezcala stone head; 7″ high.

PAGE 77: *Top:* Mezcala figurine of a man; polished green diorite; 11½″ high. Collection Mr. and Mrs. Joseph Clark III. *Bottom:* Seated figurine of black diorite; 4¼″ high.

PAGE 79: The circular pyramid at Cuicuilco.

PAGE 80: *Left and Right:* Two male pottery figurines from Tlapacoya; 5½″ and 6½″ high. Collection S. Dubiner.

PAGE 81: Two pottery ear disks from Ticoman; 1½″ diameter. AMNH.

PAGE 84: The so-called Pyramid of the Sun, at Teotihuacán, which rises to a height of 210 feet.

PAGE 88: Mural of Tlalocán, the Paradise of the Rain God, found in the painted palace of Tepantitla at Teotihuacán.

PAGE 89: Cylindrical tripod bowl of burnished brown pottery with incised designs representing rain god and his attributes; 4½″ high. Teotihuacán III style. AMNH.

PAGE 90: Citadel at Teotihuacán. This temple is a later addition to the Pyramid of Quetzalcóatl (see photograph on p. 94).

PAGE 91: Serpentine figurine, Teotihuacán III style; 2½″ high. AMNH.

PAGE 92: *Top:* Pottery figurine of dancing person in Tlalocán; 5″ high. Compare with the figurines in the mural of Tepantitla on p. 88. Collection Leo Rosshandler. *Bottom:* Giant monolithic Teotihuacán statue known as "The Water Goddess" (Chalchihuítlicue); 10′ high. MNAM.

PAGE 93: Classic Teotihuacán mask of translucent tecali (Mexican onyx); 6″ high. Incised lines below the eyes, as well as eyes and mouth themselves, were originally filled with inlays of contrasting materials. Collection Jay C. Leff.

PAGE 94: Temple of Quetzalcóatl, at Teotihuacán. Eyes of the massive serpent heads were originally inlaid with disks of polished obsidian, and the carved stonework was painted in brilliant colors.

PAGE 95: Wheeled effigy animal; 6″ long. This example was found near Remojadas, Veracruz; others have been found at Teotihuacán and elsewhere in Mexico dating from Classic times on.

PAGE 96: Teotihuacán III style lid of a funerary urn; 15″ high. AMNH.

PAGE 99: Part of the temple complex on top of Monte Albán, Oaxaca. Note the ball court on extreme left.

PAGE 100: Monte Albán I style figure of light-gray pottery; 26″ high. AMNH.

PAGE 101: *Left:* Monte Albán II effigy urn; 12″ high. AMNH. *Right:* Monte Albán I effigy urn of light-gray pottery; 8¼″ high. Collection C. B. Cohn.

PAGE 102: Elaborate urn representing Zapotec rain god Cocijo; Monte Albán III–IV; 18″ high. AMNH.

PAGE 105: *Top:* Reconstruction of Tomb 104 from Monte Albán, Period III. AMNH. *Bottom:* Newly uncovered carved stone relief at Monte Albán.

PAGE 107: *Top:* Early Classic clay figurine from Remojadas, Veracruz; 11″ high. Collection Jay C. Leff. *Bottom:* Remojadas figurine of priest; 15¼″ high. A whistle is embedded in the back of the figure.

PAGE 108: *Top:* "Smiling Head" figurine of young girl; 12½″ high. Figurines of this type were made in sections in pottery molds. Note how the same mold was used for both left and right hands. *Bottom:* "Smiling Head"; 7″ high.

PAGE 109: *Top:* Remojadas figurine standing in gate; 9″ high. *Bottom:* Two figurines on bench, with bowl; Remojadas; 8½″ high. RVVL.

PAGE 110: Remojadas effigy urn with heavy black tar decoration; 17½″ high. VMFA.

PAGE 111: Remojadas head of warrior wearing jaguar headdress; 9″ high. AMNH.

PAGE 112: Remojadas head of dignitary; 10¼″ high. Collection Dr. Paul Vignos.

PAGE 114: *Left:* Classic Veracruz figurine, showing hand-modeled details applied to mold-made basic form; 7″ high. AMNH. *Right:* Figurine on swing, from El Faisan, Veracruz; 11″ high. RVVL.

PAGE 115: Remojadas figure of seated dignitary; 15½″ high. Collection Gimpel Fils.

PAGE 117: Classic Veracruz yoke seen from above. Yoke represents a stylized frog (eyes are the quarter-rounds at top of yoke), heavily decorated with scroll-style ornaments; polished green stone; 18″ long. AMNH.

PAGE 118: Yoke end with human profile; 4″ high. AMNH.

PAGE 119: Classic Veracruz *hacha;* gray volcanic stone; 15″ high. This flat stone head is still largely covered with red paint except for an L-shaped band about 1½″ in width on lower right, where the *hacha* was originally held in place in notched setting. AMNH.

PAGE 121: *Hacha* of hard green stone showing man wearing bird headdress; 8″ high. AMNH.

PAGE 123: *Left: Palma* of gray volcanic stone; 13″ high. Note the elaborate scroll design which almost disguises rain god's two stylized mouths, from which waters are pouring out (top center and bottom center). *Right: Hacha* portraying dignitary wearing *hacha* and a supporting belt; gray volcanic stone; 28½″ high. Collection Jay C. Leff.

PAGE 125: Marble bowl from Ulúa Valley, Honduras; 8½″ high. Note face of deity in the elaborate scroll design. AMNH.

PAGE 127: Temple of Inscriptions, at Palenque. Inside pyramid on which this temple stands, tomb of a high Maya dignitary was found (see photographs, p. 135 and frontispiece).

PAGE 128: Temple of Inscriptions at Tikal.

PAGE 131: Classic Maya glyphic inscriptions.

PAGE 132: *Left:* Stela at Tikal with glyphic inscriptions. *Right:* Classic Maya stela at Tikal, showing dignitary carrying shield with face of Teotihuacán-style rain god.

PAGE 133: *Left:* Reverse of the stela shown on p. 132 (right). Note dignitary holding long chain. His face is smashed, as is face of the figure on obverse side. *Right:* Classic Maya carved wood panels found at Tikal.

PAGE 135: Burial chamber found inside pyramid of Temple of Inscriptions at Palenque. This enormous stone slab covered sarcophagus itself. Note "Tree of Life" on upper part of slab. Reconstruction in the MNAM.

PAGE 136: Three emerald green Maya jade pendants, from Toniná, Chiapas. AMNH. *Top:* A pendant recut from an earlier object; 2¼″ high. *Center:* Large jade bead; 2⅛″ diameter. Glyph is one of three incised at even intervals on bead; one glyph has been read as the Maya date 9.15.0.0.0., which falls in A.D. 731. *Bottom:* Jade plaque showing seated dignitary; 4″ high.

PAGE 137: Maya pottery figurine from Jaina island; 7″ high. Figurines of this type were originally painted in brilliant colors; heavy traces of "Maya blue" often survive.

PAGE 138: Maya mold-made figurine with hand-modeled headdress; 6½″ high. Collection Mr. and Mrs. Daniel Rose.

PAGE 140: Detail of murals found at Bonampak, showing a procession. Reconstruction at MNAM.

PAGE 141: Detail of Bonampak mural showing a battle scene. Note richly caparisoned victors and primitively dressed vanquished warriors. Reconstruction at MNAM.

PAGE 143: *Left:* Teotihuacán-style tripod bowl with effigy-head lid found at Tikal. *Right:* Maya incised bowl found near Uxmal; 7″ high. Seated figurine is seen having his face painted with symbolic designs by another personage to left. AMNH.

PAGE 145: *Top:* Polychrome plate from Jaina island; 11″ diameter. AMNH. *Bottom:* Polychrome bowl, Yucatan; 7″ high. AMNH.

PAGE 146: Typical corbeled Maya archway.

PAGE 147: Late Classic Maya graffito on fired brick, found in palace at Comalcalco, Tabasco. AMNH.

PAGE 148: Temple of the Cross, at Palenque. Note typical roof comb on top of this temple, which derives its name from the cross-shaped Tree of Life relief found in back of sanctuary.

PAGE 150: West range of "Nunnery" quadrangle at Uxmal.

PAGE 151: Late Classic Maya buildings at Chichén Itzá: "Nunnery" on the left, "Iglesia" on the right. Note typical Puuc-style masks of the long-snouted rain god on right.

PAGE 152: "Tablet of the Slaves," a wall relief in the palace at Palenque. Note elaborate headdress being offered to dignitary seated on double-headed jaguar throne.

PAGE 153: The Observatory at Chichén Itzá.

PAGE 155: *Top:* Huaxtec II pottery figurine; 4″ high. *Bottom:* Huaxtec III figurine; 12″ high. Collection Michael D. Coe.

PAGE 156: Stone statue, "Adolescent Boy," found near Tamuin; Huaxtec V period; 4′ 4″ high.

PAGE 157: Detail of back of "Adolescent Boy" (see photograph, p. 156).

PAGE 163: Detail of mural found at ball court at Tajín.

PAGE 164: Pyramid of the Niches at Tajín; about 60′ high.

PAGE 167: Detail of stone relief surrounding base of temple at Xochicalco, showing a seated dignitary.

PAGE 169: Toltec Mayapán-style mold-made pottery deity effigy; 7″ high. AMNH.

PAGE 171: Main pyramid at Tula.

PAGE 173: Giant atlantean stone figures surmounting pyramid at Tula; 18′ high. Each figure is made of four fitted sections of stone. They represent warriors carrying *atlatl* (throwing stick) in one hand and bag for copal incense in the other. On chest of each man is the Toltec emblem, a stylized butterfly pectoral.

PAGE 174: Temple of Warriors, at Chichén Itzá, seen from the base of the stairway of the Temple of Kukulcán. Note columns in front of temple; originally they were roofed and served to hold great assemblages of warriors and other participants in temple ceremonies.

PAGE 175: Figure of a Chac-Mool; gray volcanic stone; 12½″ long. This example of the deity usually associated with the Maya-Toltec period was excavated in the Tarascan capital of Tzintzuntzan, Michoacán. AMNH.

PAGE 175: Base of *tzompantli* (skull rack) at Chichén Itzá.

PAGE 176: Temple of Warriors at Chichén Itzá. Note serpent column and masks of long-

nosed rain god applied to temple walls.

PAGE 177: Life-size Toltec pottery figure representing god Xipe-Totec dressed in the skin of human victim. AMNH.

PAGE 178: Plumbate effigy vase of the Old Man God, Huehueteotl. Reproduced actual size. AMNH.

PAGE 181: Chichén Itzá: Pyramid of Kukulcán seen from Temple of Warriors. Note Chac-Mool figure in right foreground, serpent head of snake column on left. In center is the Toltec warrior standard-bearer on temple steps.

PAGE 185: Toltec Mayapán-style effigy head of brown pottery with red decorations; 7″ high. AMNH.

PAGE 189: Two late Maya mold-made articulated pottery figurines of warriors, from Jaina island; 12½″ and 13¼″ high. This type of figurine with movable limbs first appears at Teotihuacán (see p. 95). Collection Jay C. Leff, and Olsen Collection, Yale University Art Gallery.

PAGE 193: Mixtec polychrome bowl with *xicalcoliuhqui* stepped-key design; 5½″ high. AMNH.

PAGES 194-95: Four pages from Codex Vaticanus "B." This codex contains a *tonalámatl*, the calendar of the 260-day religious year. Each of the four pages shown depicts a different appearance of the rain god. Band across top is filled with sky and rain symbols; glyphs on bottom band represent calendar days under the particular deity's protection. Each page measures 5½ x 6 inches, and the 49 pages of the complete codex stretch to a length of 24½ feet.

PAGE 196: Page from the Codex Nuttall; 7½″ × 10″. Scene represents three historical persons approaching mountain on left; lower panel is filled with water creatures.

PAGE 197: Mixtec polychrome tripod bowl with snake effigy feet; 11″ high. AMNH.

PAGE 198: Mixtec deity figurine (*penate*) of tecali (Mexican onyx); 4⅛″ high. Note double serpent headdress. Collection Eugene Berman.

PAGE 199: Monkey effigy vessel of tecali; 10″ high. MAI—HF.

PAGE 200: Three Mixtec-style gold ornaments. AMNH. Note the use of bells in ring and on ear plug. Eagle-head labret in center is 2″ long; it was worn as a plug through lower lip. AMNH.

PAGE 201: Mixtec gold labret; 2¾″ long. The snake's tongue is movable. AMNH.

PAGE 202: Portion of inner walls of Palace II at Mitla. Note typically Mixtec *xicalcoliuhqui* stepped-key design.

PAGE 204: Mixtec polychrome pottery effigy vase of Macuilxochitl ("Five Flowers"), god of games and feasting. Found at Mihuatlan, Oaxaca; 12″ high. AMNH.

PAGE 205: *Left:* North façade of Building of the Columns, Mitla. Note extraordinary length of stone lintels across each entrance way. *Right:* Interior of Building of the Columns, Mitla.

PAGE 212: Animal effigy vessel from Misantla, Veracruz; white, red and black paint on tan pottery; 10″ high. AMNH.

PAGE 213: Plate with stylized serpent head from Misantla, Veracruz; white and brown paint on tan pottery; 11″ diameter. AMNH.

PAGE 215: Aztec *teponatzli* (wooden drum); 19″ long. AMNH.

PAGE 216: Aztec kneeling stone figure; 20″ high. AMNH.

PAGE 221: Aztec stone figure of a *Cihuateteo*, a woman who died in childbirth; 26″ high. AMNH.

PAGE 223: Aztec stone figure of a female deity reflected in an Aztec obsidian mirror with carved wooden frame. Diameter of frame 10¼″. AMNH.

PAGE 224: Aztec temple model showing a Sun Disk installed on a platform. This monolith is known as the National Stone because on the back it is carved with the Aztec symbol—an eagle with a serpent in his beak, standing on a *nopal* cactus—which is also the coat of arms of modern Mexico. MNAM.

PAGE 225: The famous 13-foot Sun Disk often referred to as the Calendar Stone. MNAM.

PAGE 226: Memorial stone to the Aztec emperor Tizoc, recording his victories; 9′ diameter. MNAM.

PAGE 227: Colossal statue of Coatlicue, Mother of the Gods; more than 8′ high. Her fearsome attributes include a head consisting of two snakes which rise from her neck, and hands and feet tipped with giant claws to help her feed on human corpses. The goddess wears a skirt of writhing snakes and a necklace strung with human hearts and hands, with a human skull as center pendant. MNAM.

PAGE 228: Kneeling figurine of a Water Goddess; gray volcanic stone, 11″ high. Note the *quexquemitl*, a cape which is still being made and worn by Mexican Indian women. AMNH.

PAGE 229: *Top:* Aztec grasshopper of red diorite; 18″ long. MNAM. *Bottom:* Aztec calabash of green diorite; 12″ long. MNAM.

PAGE 231: Aztec-IV-style tripod plate with *molcajete* grid for grinding peppers; 8″ diameter. AMNH.

PAGE 237: Aztec mask of green diorite; 7⅛″ high. Found at Castillo de Teayo, Veracruz, a fortified military outpost of the Aztec empire. AMNH.

SOME BOOKS FOR FURTHER READING

Books which the general reader may find particularly useful for further introductory reading are noted with an asterisk (*), while those which are especially interesting for their reproductions and illustrations are marked with a dagger (†). Because reading knowledge of Spanish, French and German is so widespread today, a number of important and helpful works in these languages have been included in this suggested reading list.

Serious students and readers with special interests in one or another aspect of Middle American art and archaeology are referred to the authoritative and exhaustive bibliography recently compiled by Ignacio Bernal, *Bibliografía de arqueología y etnografía,* and to the bibliography in Raúl Noriega and others, *Esplendor del México antiguo,* both of which are listed below.

† Ashton, Dore, and Boltin, Lee, *Abstract Art before Columbus.* New York: André Emmerich Gallery, 1957.
* Bernal, Ignacio, *Bibliografía de arqueología y etnografía, Mesoamérica y Norte de México.* Mexico City: Instituto Nacional de Antropología e Historia, 1962.

* ———, *Tenochtitlán en una isla.* Mexico City: Instituto Nacional de Antropología e Historia, 1959.

† ——— and Soustelle, Jacques, *Mexico: Pre-Hispanic Paintings.* Greenwich, Conn.: New York Graphic Society, by arrangement with UNESCO, 1958.

† Bird, Junius B., and Ekholm, Gordon F., *Pre-Columbian Gold Sculpture.* New York: Museum of Primitive Art, 1959.

† Burland, Cottie A., *Magic Books from Mexico.* Harmondsworth, Middlesex: Penguin Books, 1953.

Caso, Alfonso, *The Aztecs, People of the Sun.* Norman, Okla.: University of Oklahoma Press, 1958.

——— and Bernal, Ignacio, *Urnas de Oaxaca.* Mexico City: Instituto Nacional de Antropología e Historia, Memorias, Vol. 2, 1952.

Coe, Michael D., *Mexico.* New York: Frederick A. Praeger, 1962.

Covarrubias, Miguel, *The Eagle, the Jaguar and the Serpent* (Indian Art of the Americas: North America). New York: Alfred A. Knopf, 1954.

* ———, *Indian Art of Mexico and Central America.* New York: Alfred A. Knopf, 1957.

———, *Mexico South: The Isthmus of Tehuantepec.* New York: Alfred A. Knopf, 1946.

† ———, *Mezcala: Ancient Mexican Sculpture.* New York: André Emmerich Gallery, 1956.

* Díaz del Castillo, Bernal, *The Discovery and Conquest of Mexico, 1517–1521.* New York: Farrar, Straus & Cudahy, 1956; Grove Press, 1958.

Easby, Dudley T., Jr., "Ancient American Goldsmiths," *Natural History Magazine,* Vol. LXV, No. 8 (October 1956).

Ekholm, Gordon F., "Excavations at Tampico and Pánuco in the Huaxteca, Mexico," *Anthropological Papers, American Museum of Natural History,* Vol. 38, Part 5 (1944).

———, "The Probable Use of Stone Yokes," *American Anthropologist,* Vol. 48, No. 4 (1945).

———, "Wheeled Toys in Mexico," *American Antiquity,* Vol. 2, No. 4 (1946).

———, "Palmate Stones and Thin Stone Heads," *American Antiquity,* Vol. 15, No. 1 (1949).

† ———, *Stone Sculpture from Mexico.* New York: Museum of Primitive Art, 1959.

Emmerich, André, "Savages Never Carved These Stones," *American Heritage,* Vol. X, No. 2 (February 1959).

† Groth Kimball, Irmgard, *Maya Terracottas.* New York: Frederick A. Praeger, 1961.

† ——— and Feuchtwanger, Franz, *The Art of Ancient Mexico.* New York and London: Thames & Hudson, 1954.

Heine Geldern, Robert, and Ekholm, Gordon F., "Significant Parallels in the Symbolic Arts of Southern Asia and Middle America," *Selected Papers of the XXIXth International Congress of Americanists,* Chicago, 1951.

† Kelemen, Pál, *Medieval American Art.* New York: Macmillan, 1943, 1960.

† Kidder, Alfred V., and Samayoa Chinchilla, Carlos, *The Art of Ancient Maya.* New York: Thomas Y. Crowell, 1959.

* Krickeberg, Walter, *Altmexikanische Kulturen.* Berlin: Safari-Verlag, 1956.

† Kubler, George, *The Louise and Walter Arensberg Collection,* Vol. II, *Pre-Columbian Sculpture.* Philadelphia Museum of Art, 1954.

† Kutscher, Gerhardt K., Lothrop, Samuel K., and Gamboa, Fernando, *Kunst der Mexikaner.* Zurich: Kunsthaus, 1959.

Lehmann, Henri, *Les Céramiques précolombiennes.* Paris: Presses universitaires de France, L'Oeil du Connaisseur, 1959.

† Linné, Sigveld, *Treasures of Mexican Art.* Stockholm: Nordisk Rotogravyr, 1956.

Lothrop, Samuel Kirkland, "Metals from the Cenote of Sacrifice, Chichén Itzá Yucatán," *Peabody Museum Memoirs,* Harvard University, Vol. X, No. 2 (1952).

† ———, Foshag, W. F., and Mahler, Joy, *Pre-Columbian Art: The Robert Woods Bliss Collection.* New York: Phaidon, 1957.

Médioni, Gilbert, *L'Art tarasque du Mexique occidental.* Paris: Paul Hartmann, 1952.

† ——— and Pinto, Marie-Thérèse, *Art in Ancient Mexico* (selected and photographed from the collection of Diego Rivera). New York: Oxford University Press, 1941.

* Morley, Sylvanus Griswold, and Brainerd, George W., *The Ancient Maya.* Stanford, Calif.: Stanford University Press, 1956.

* Noriega, Raúl, Cook de Leonard, Carmen, and Moctezuma, Julio Rodolfo, with 48 contributors, *Esplendor del México antiguo*, 2v. Mexico City: Centro de Investigaciones Antropologicas de México, 1959.

Peterson, Frederick A., *Ancient Mexico*. New York: Putnam, 1959.

† Piña Chán, Román, *Tlatilco*, 2v. Mexico City: Instituto Nacional de Antropología e Historia, 1958.

————, *Mesoamérica*. Mexico City: Instituto Nacional de Antropología e Historia, 1960.

† Proskouriakoff, Tatiana, *An Album of Maya Architecture*. Washington, D.C.: Carnegie Institution of Washington, Publication 558, 1946.

————, *A Study of Classic Maya Sculpture*. Washington, D.C.: Carnegie Institution of Washington, Publication 593, 1950.

† ————, *Varieties of Classic Central Veracruz Sculpture*. Washington, D.C.: Carnegie Institution of Washington, Publication 606, 1954.

† Ruppert, Karl, Thompson, J. Eric S., and Proskouriakoff, Tatiana, *Bonampak, Chiapas, Mexico*. Washington, D.C.: Carnegie Institution of Washington, Publication 602, 1955.

Sahagún, Fray Bernardino de, *Historia general de las cosas de Nueva España*. Mexico City: Edición Porrua, 1956.

————, *General History of the Things of New Spain* [9v.]: *Florentine Codex*. Monographs of the School of American Research, No. 14. Santa Fe, N.M.: 1950–1959.

Soustelle, Jacques, *La Vie quotidienne des aztèques*. Paris: Librairie Hachette, 1955 (illustrated edition, 1959).

† Spratling, William, *More Human Than Divine*. Mexico City: Universidad Nacional Autónoma de México, 1960.

* Thompson, J. Eric S., *The Rise and Fall of Maya Civilization*. Norman, Okla.: University of Oklahoma Press, 1954.

Toscano, Salvador, *Arte precolombino de México y de la América central*. Mexico City: Universidad Nacional Autónoma de México, 1952.

† ————, Kirchhoff, Paul, and Rubin de la Borbolla, Daniel F., *Arte precolombino del Occidente de México*. Mexico City: Secretería de Educación Pública, 1946.

* Vaillant, George C., *The Aztecs of Mexico*. Garden City, N.Y.: Doubleday, 1944. London: Pelican Books, 1950.

GLOSSARY

ANTHROPOMORPHIC: Having the figure of a man; in the image of a human being. Thus, axes carved in the likeness of a man are referred to as anthropomorphic axes.

ARCHAIC: In pre-Columbian art, usually used to refer to the Preclassic Period (*circa* 1500–200 B.C.) and its art style.

CARYATID: A human figure supporting a beam or lintel.

CELT: A stone shaped like a chisel or an ax.

CINNABAR: A red color derived from mercuric sulphide.

COCHINEAL: A red dyestuff made of the dried bodies of the females of a scale insect known as the cochineal insect.

CODEX (*plural*, CODICES): Ancient manuscript. In Mexico, this term refers primarily to Indian picture-writing manuscripts made during pre-Conquest and earliest post-Conquest times.

FRESCO: Wall painting in which pigments are applied with water as a vehicle on a lime ground.

GRAFFITO (*plural*, GRAFFITI): Rudely scratched figures and inscriptions.

HIERATIC STYLE: Art made according to strict canons imposed by a priestly ruling elite and dedicated to glorifying an established divine and social order.

ICONOGRAPHIC: Iconography is the science of symbolism, of reading the meaning of art forms. Thus, iconographic ornamentation is ornamentation using images and pictures which are a kind of symbolic shorthand representing complicated concepts readily comprehended only by initiates.

KAOLIN: Very pure, white clay, a hydrous silicate of aluminum, used in modern times for making white porcelain.

NEGATIVE PAINT DECORATION: A method where only the background of the design to be reproduced is filled in with color, permitting the original surface to represent the design itself. Usually done by the *resist painting* method in which the design is painted on with a material such as wax which projects the original surface and resists the process to which the pottery or fabric is then submitted, such as dipping in paint or smoking above a fire. The resist material is then scraped off, revealing the original surface which now forms the design.

PASTILLAJE: A Spanish term, literally "pill making." Used in archaeology to describe a method for making pottery figurines in which such elements as eyes, nose, headdress, ornaments, are made up of small pellets of clay applied to the basic form of the figure.

PICTOGRAPHIC. Referring to picture writing.

POTSHERD: Also shard or sherd: fragment of a pottery vessel or figure.

RELIEF: Projection of figures from a background. According to the degree of projection, *high relief* is half or more than half of natural projection; *low relief* or *bas relief* is slight, no part being entirely detached from the background.

REPOUSSÉ: Metal formed in relief, decorated by hammering and pressing from the obverse, usually over a pattern.

SLIP: A process used in making clay figurines and vessels in which a fine clay is applied in a liquid state as decorative surface material.

STELE (*plural*, STELAE): A Greek term for a slab or pillar-like monument. Commonly used in archaeology.

STUCCO: A building material made of a plaster-lime compound, used in a plastic state, usually to form decorations on exterior surfaces of buildings.

INDEX